A-LEVEL CH

FLASH NOTES

AQA YEAR 2

New Syllabus 2015

Dr C. Boes

Condensed Revision Notes (Flashcards) for Successful Exam Preparation

Designed to Facilitate Memorization

www.alevelchemistryrevision.co.uk

Text copyright © 2015 Dr. Christoph Boes

All rights reserved

Cover Image copyright © Pedro Antonio Salaverría Calahorra
Dreamstime.com (Image ID: 13534535)
http://www.dreamstime.com/pedro2009_info

All other Images copyright © 2015 Dr. Christoph Boes

Self-published 2016

ISBN-13: 978-0995706040

Table of Contents

Unit 1 – Physical Chemistry 7
1.8 Thermodynamics 7
Born-Haber Cycle 7
Enthalpy Change of Solution 9
Entropy 11
Free Energy 13

1.9 Rate Equations 15
Rates 15
Rate Constant k & Rate Determining Step 17
Concentration-Time Graphs & Half-Life 19
Rate-Concentration Graphs 21
Iodine Clock 23
Arrhenius Equation 25

1.10 Gas Equilibrium 27
Gas Equilibrium 27

1.11 Electrode Potentials 29
Electrode Potentials 29
Redox Equations 31
Calculating Voltages of Cells & Applications 33

1.12 Acids, Bases and Buffers 35
Strong Acids and Bases 35
Weak Acids 37
Buffers 39
Buffer Example Calculations 41
Titration Curves I 43
Titration Curves II 45

Unit 2 – Inorganic Chemistry 47
2.4 Properties of Period 3 Elements 47
Properties of Period 3 Elements 47

2.5 Transition Metals 49
Redox Titrations 49
Example Calculation – Redox Titration 51
Transition Elements 53
Complexes 55
Stereoisomerism in Transition Metal Complexes 57

2.6 Reactions of Transition Metals Ions 59
Reactions of Transition Metal Ions 59

Unit 3 - Organic Chemistry ... 61

3.7 Optical Isomers ... 61
Optical Isomers ... 61

3.8 Aldehydes & Ketones ... 63
Aldehydes & Ketones ... 63

3.9 Carboxylic Acids and Esters ... 65
Carboxylic Acids & Anhydrides ... 65
Esters ... 67
Fats & Oils ... 69
Acyl Chlorides ... 71

3.10 Aromatic Compounds ... 73
Benzene & Arenes ... 73
Reactions of Arenes ... 75

3.11 Amines ... 77
Amines ... 77
Preparation of Amines & Amides ... 79

3.12 Condensation Polymers ... 81
Condensation Polymers ... 81
Important Polymers ... 83

3.13 Amino Acids, Proteins and DNA ... 85
Amino Acids & Proteins ... 85
DNA & Tests for Functional Groups ... 87

3.14 Organic Synthesis ... 89
Preparation and Purification of Organic Compounds ... 89

3.15 NMR ... 91
NMR Spectroscopy: H-NMR & Carbon 13-NMR ... 91
How to predict NMR Spectrum from Structural Formula ... 93

3.16 Chromatography ... 95
Thin Layer Chromatography ... 95
Gas Chromatography & Column Chromatography ... 97
Tips for Organic Synthesis & Combined Techniques Questions ... 99

Appendix: Periodic Table of Elements ... 101

How to use these notes

Revision notes (revision cards) are an effective and successful way to prepare for exams. They contain the necessary exam knowledge in a condensed, easy to memorize form. These notes are designed for the final stage of revision and require a thorough understanding of the topics. If this understanding is lacking then help from a professional tutor and additional study of text books or revision guides is suggested.

These revision notes are organized in chapters according to the new 2015 AQA Year 2 syllabus. Each chapter contains individual revision cards covering all the necessary topics. Everything in *italic* is optional knowledge, aimed at students who want to excel or want to continue with chemistry at university. **Bold** represents important keywords or key definitions. *'Data sheet'* indicates information which will be provided on the data sheet during the exam and does not need to be memorized. Important information and exam-specific tips are highlighted in yellow.

How to memorize: - The revision cards are introduced by their titles and keywords on a separate page. After reading the title you should try to write down the content of the card without looking at the next page. The keywords give you hints about the content. Write down everything you remember, even if you are not sure. Then check if your answers are correct; if not, rewrite the incorrect ones.
At the beginning, when you are still unfamiliar with the cards, it might help to read them a few times first. If they contain a lot of content, you can cover the revision card with a piece of paper and slowly reveal the header and sub content. While you uncover it try to remember what is written in the covered part, e.g. the definition for a term you just uncovered. This uncovering technique is for the early stages, later you should be able to write down the whole content after just reading the header. If this is the case, move to the next card. If not, bookmark the card and memorize it repeatedly. Do at least three to four sessions per week until you know all the cards in one chapter word-perfectly. Then move on to the next section. Generally it is better to do shorter sessions more often than longer sessions less frequently.
An even better option is to ask somebody to check your knowledge by reading the header aloud and comparing your answer to the content. Alternatively, get together in learning groups and support each other. Discuss topics which you don't understand; your friend might know the answers or ask your teacher or tutor. More tips about revision techniques and exam resources can be found on my website: http://www.alevelchemistryrevision.co.uk

Disclaimer: Due to the changing nature of mark schemes it cannot be guaranteed that answering according to these notes will give you full marks. These notes constitute only one part of a full revision program and work alongside other methods, like practising past papers. They have been created with great care; however, it cannot be guaranteed there are no errors or omissions.

Unit 1 – Physical Chemistry

1.8 Thermodynamics

Born-Haber Cycle

Purpose
Definition of lattice enthalpy
Characteristics of lattice enthalpy (three points)
Definition of lattice dissociation enthalpy
Equation for lattice enthalpy
Example with enthalpies and equations
Tip
Difference between theoretical and experimental lattice enthalpies

Born-Haber Cycle

-> to calculate lattice enthalpy of a salt (application of Hess's law)

Lattice enthalpy
Definition: Enthalpy given off when **gaseous ions** form **1 mole** of an **ionic solid** (salt) under standard conditions **(298K, 100 kPa)**. **-> always negative**

- to estimate the strength of bonds in an ionic compound (salt)
  -> determines it's physical characteristics (solubility, melting point)
- higher charge, smaller ions => lattice enthalpy increases (electrostatic)
- often cannot be measured (very exothermic) -> indirect approach
  => Born-Haber splits the process of forming a salt from its elements (standard states) in small steps, which can be measured or calculated

Lattice dissociation energy (reverse of lattice energy) $\Delta H^\ominus_{diss} = -\Delta H^\ominus_{latt}$
Definition: Enthalpy change to separate 1 mol of an ionic substance into its gaseous ions. **(positive)**

$$\text{Hess's law:} \quad \Delta H^\ominus_{latt} = \Delta H^\ominus_f - \Delta H^\ominus_{others}$$

$\Delta H^\ominus_{latt}$: standard lattice enthalpy
$\Delta H^\ominus_f$: standard enthalpy of formation
$\Delta H^\ominus_{others}$: Σ enthalpies transforming elements into gaseous ions: atomisation + ionisation + affinity enthalpies

Example:
$$Na_{(s)} + ½ Cl_{2(g)} \rightarrow NaCl_{(s)}$$

$\Delta H^\ominus_{at}$: **standard enthalpy of atomization** $Na_{(s)} \rightarrow Na_{(g)}$
= ½ bond dissociation enthalpy
E_{I1}:   **first ionization energy** $Na_{(g)} \rightarrow Na^+ + e^-$
=> remove electrons stepwise (1st and 2nd ionisation), never 2 moles e⁻ at the same time
$\Delta H^\ominus_{at}$: **standard enthalpy of atomization** $½ Cl_{2(g)} \rightarrow Cl_{(g)}$
E_{aff}:   **electron affinity** $Cl_{(g)} + e^- \rightarrow Cl^-_{(g)}$
    First electron affinity is exothermic (-): $O_{(g)} + e^- \rightarrow O^-_{(g)}$
    Second affinity is endothermic (e⁻ to O⁻) $O^-(g) + e^- \rightarrow O^{2-}(g)$
$\Delta H^\ominus_{latt}$: **standard lattice energy** $Na^+_{(g)} + Cl^-_{(g)} \rightarrow NaCl_{(s)}$

-> memorize Year 1 revision card 'Enthalpy changes - Definition'

$$\Delta H^\ominus_{latt} = \Delta H^\ominus_f - \Delta H^\ominus_{others}$$

$$\Delta H^\ominus_{latt} = \Delta H^\ominus_f - (\Delta H^\ominus_{at}[Na_{(s)}] + E_{I1}[Na_{(g)}] + \Delta H^\ominus_{at}[Cl_{(g)}] + E_{aff}[Cl_{(g)}])$$

Make sure you multiply $\Delta H^\ominus_{at}$ and E_{aff} by two for salts with formula MX₂

The more polarization of the ionic bond the more degree of covalent bond instead of ideal ionic bond
 => explains why **experimental lattice energies (Born-Haber) are higher than theoretical ones** (Coulomb's law, ideal ions -> point charges; covalent bond stronger than ionic)

Enthalpy Change of Solution

Definition for enthalpy change of solution
Equation for enthalpy change of solution
Energetic conditions for a salt to be soluble
Definition for enthalpy change of hydration
Characteristics of hydration enthalpy (four points)
Equation to calculate enthalpy change of hydration
Example calculation

Enthalpy change of solution $\Delta H_{solution}$

Definition: Enthalpy change when 1 mole of a substance is completely dissolved under standard conditions

Dissolving consists of two competing processes:
1) hydration of ion releases energy (exothermic -)
2) breaking up the lattice requires energy (endothermic +)

$$\Delta H_{solution} = \Delta H_{hyd} - \Delta H_{latt}$$

The lattice enthalpy ΔH_{latt} (energy released when salt formed) is exothermic (-), therefore sign in front of ΔH_{latt} becomes positive (-- = +)

=> $\Delta H_{solution}$ must be **negative** ($\Delta H_{hyd} > \Delta H_{latt}$) or slightly positive (due to increased entropy) for a salt to be soluble

Enthalpy change of hydration ΔH_{hyd}

Definition: Enthalpy change when 1 mole of gaseous ions form aqueous ions (dissolve) under standard conditions

- increases with charge density of ion (smaller ion, higher charge)
- exothermic: electrostatic attraction between ion and dipole water
  -> **ion-dipole bonds**
- it is a theoretical value (gaseous phase), but can be calculated with the equation below (Hess's law), since $\Delta H_{solution}$ can easily be measured:

$$\Delta H_{hyd} = \Delta H_{solution} + \Delta H_{latt}$$

- **add hydration enthalpies of each ion to get hydration enthalpy of the whole salt**

$$\Delta H_{hyd} (CaCl_2) = \Delta H_{hyd} (Ca^{2+}) + 2 \times \Delta H_{hyd} (Cl^-)$$

-> use Gibbs equation to calculate if salt is soluble at a given temperature (see revision card 'Entropy')

Example

Calculate if $CaCl_2$ is soluble in water, by using the data below.
$\Delta H_{hyd}(Ca^{2+})$:   -1579 kJ mol^{-1}
$\Delta H_{hyd}(Cl^-)$:   -364 kJ mol^{-1}
$\Delta H_{latt}(CaCl_2)$:   -2255 kJ mol^{-1}

$\Delta H_{solution} = \Delta H_{hyd} - \Delta H_{latt}$
$\Delta H_{solution} = [-1579 + (2 \times -364)] - (-2255)$ | kJ mol^{-1}
$\Delta H_{solution} = \quad -52$ kJ mol^{-1}

=> $\Delta H_{solution}$ is **negative**, therefore $CaCl_2$ should be soluble in water

Entropy

Definition

Entropy depends on… (three points)

Equation for ΔS_{sys} with rule

If entropy increases then sign for ΔS is…

Equation for ΔS_{total}

Equation for ΔS_{surr}

Tip

Example

Entropy

Definition: Randomness or disorder of a system

Entropy depends on:

   I) Physical State: solid < liquid < gases
                          -> increasing freedom of movement & disorder
                          => increasing entropy (positive)

   II) Temperature: increasing temperature -> increasing entropy

   III) Number of Moles: Increasing number of moles -> increasing entropy

Entropy change in a chemical reaction

$$\Delta S_{sys} = \Sigma S_{prod} - \Sigma S_{react}$$

ΔS_{sys}: entropy change of the reaction [J K^{-1} mol^{-1}]
S: molar entropies (of products or reactants)

-> Multiply S by mole numbers from mole-equation

If the system loses energy by increasing the entropy then the sign for $+\Delta S$ is positive -> contrary to the negative sign for exothermic reactions: $-\Delta H$

-> *Entropy is a form of energy*

Total entropy change of reaction

$$\Delta S_{total} = \Delta S_{sys} + \Delta S_{surr}$$

-> includes entropy of surroundings (ΔS_{surr}) in an open system (energy exchange with surroundings)
-> *if ΔS_{total} is positive then the reaction will happen spontaneously*

$$\Delta S_{surr} = -\frac{\Delta H}{T}$$

T: temperature in Kelvin (0 °C = 273 K)
ΔH: enthalpy change of reaction [J mol^{-1}] **(often given in KJ -> convert!)**
-> ΔS_{surr} will be positive for exothermic reactions $-\Delta H$: -- => +

Example:
$$2NO_{2(g)} \rightleftharpoons 1N_2O_{4(g)}$$

S (N$_2$O$_4$): 304 J K^{-1} mol^{-1}
S (NO$_2$): 240 J K^{-1} mol^{-1}

$\Delta S_{sys} = 304 - (2 \times 240) = -176$ J K^{-1} mol^{-1}
-> decrease of entropy because of fewer gas moles on product side

Free Energy

Gibbs equation with tip

For a reaction to occur spontaneously ΔG must be....

To calculate temperature for spontaneous reaction set ΔG to...

Different combinations of exothermic/endothermic ΔH with ΔS

A reaction with negative ΔG might not happen due to....

Example calculation

Free energy

Gibbs equation

$$\Delta G = \Delta H - T\Delta S$$

ΔG: free energy change of the system (reaction) [J mol^{-1}]
ΔH: enthalpy change of the reaction [**J mol^{-1}**] (**often given in KJ -> convert!**)
ΔS: entropy change of the reaction ΔS_{sys} [J K^{-1} mol^{-1}]
T: temperature [Kelvin]

=> ΔG must be negative for reaction to occur spontaneously (feasible)
-> set $\Delta G = 0$ to calculate minimum temperature for spontaneous reaction

- For an exothermic reaction (-ΔH) and a positive ΔS: TΔS adds to the free energy value because the sign before TΔS stays negative
- For an exothermic reaction and negative ΔS: TΔS subtracts from the free energy value because the sign becomes positive (+ TΔS)
- For an endothermic reaction (+ΔH) and positive ΔS: TΔS subtracts from the energy value (If TΔS > ΔH then ΔG becomes negative: an endothermic reaction can happen spontaneously)

-> A reaction with negative ΔG still might not happen spontaneously due to slow kinetics

Example Calculation

Calculate the free energy change of the following reaction at room temperature under standard pressure.

$$NH_{3(g)} + HCl_{(g)} \leftrightarrows NH_4Cl_{(s)}$$

ΔH_f (NH$_3$):   -44 kJ mol^{-1}
ΔH_f (HCl):   -94 kJ mol^{-1}
ΔH_f (NH$_4$Cl) -310 kJ mol^{-1}

S(NH$_3$):   188 J K^{-1} mol^{-1}
S(HCl):   190 J K^{-1} mol^{-1}
S(NH$_4$Cl):   98 J K^{-1} mol^{-1}

$\Delta H_r^{\ominus} = -310 - (-44 + -94) = -172$ **kJ** mol^{-1}
$\Delta S^{\ominus}_{sys} = 98 - (188 + 190) = -280$ J K^{-1} mol^{-1}

$\Delta G = \Delta H - T\Delta S$
$\Delta G = -172,000$ **J** $- (298$ K $\times -280$ J K^{-1} mol^{-1})
$\Delta G = -88,560$ J mol^{-1}

=> The reaction will be spontaneous because ΔG is negative

At a higher temperature ΔG might become positive and the reaction will not happen spontaneously anymore.

1.9 Rate Equations

Rates

Definition with equation
Rate Equation with four points and tip
Orders in respect to reactants (three points)
Overall order (two points)

Rates (Speed of reaction)

Rate of reaction: change of concentration (of products or reactants) over time

$$r = \frac{\Delta c}{\Delta t}$$

    r: rate of reaction [**mol dm^{-3} s^{-1}**]
    Δc: change of concentration
    Δt: time interval

-> Rate depends on temperature; surface area; catalyst and **concentration of reactants** (pressure for gases) -> see Year 1 revision card

$$aA + bB \rightarrow cC + dD$$

Rate equation:

$$\text{rate} = k\,[A]^m\,[B]^n$$

    k: **rate constant**
    [ ]: **concentration**
    m: **order with respect to reactant A**
    n: **order with respect to reactant B**

- Rate equation indicates how much the rate of the reaction depends on the concentrations of the reactants
- Can be used to calculate rate of reaction
- Products C, D do not appear in the rate equation because rate does not depend on product concentration, just reactants (collision theory: higher concentration -> collisions more likely)
- Catalyst (H$^+$) can appear in the rate equation (might not appear in reaction equation)
- => **rate equation has nothing to do with an equilibrium equation or the mole equation of the overall chemical reaction**

Orders m, n:
- 0 order in respect to A: rate of reaction does not depend on concentration of [A]: double [A] -> no change in rate of reaction
- 1st order in respect to A: double [A] -> rate doubles
- 2nd order in respect to A: double [A] -> rate quadruples

Overall (total) order of reactions: m+n
- **Order of reaction indicates how many of the reactants are involved in the rate determining step (1st: one reactant, 2nd: two reactants)**
- Order of reactants/reactions is determined empirically (experimentally): Concentration-Time graphs & Rate-Concentration graphs

Rate Constant k
&
Rate Determining Step

Properties of k (two points)

Applications

Units of k

Equation to calculate units of k

Definition of rate-determining step

Relationship between moles of rate determining step and order

Two rules for rate determining step and reactants

Rate equation from single steps with example

Rate constant k

- the larger k, the faster the reaction
- **k only temperature dependent**
  -> collision theory (kinetic energy > activation energy)
- applications: industry and enzymes
- units of k change depending on order

Calculate k and its units:

$$k = \frac{rate}{[A]^m[B]^n}$$

Example for unit calculation:

first order reaction: rate = k [A]

$$k = \frac{r}{[A]} = \frac{\cancel{mol\ dm^{-3}}\ s^{-1}}{\cancel{mol\ dm^{-3}}} = s^{-1}$$

Rate-determining step

Definition: slowest step in a multistep reaction

Mole equation of the rate determining step indicates the order of the reactants in the rate equation and vice versa:

$1 CH_3Cl + 1 OH^- \rightarrow CH_3OH + Cl^-$ slow (rate determining step)

rate = $k[CH_3Cl]^1[HO^-]^1$

Rules:
- If a reactant is in the rate equation, it or a species derived from it, takes part in the rate-determining step.
- If a reactant is not in the rate equation, it or a species derived from it, **does not** take part in the rate-determining step.

The reactant of the rate determining step might not be a reactant of the overall reaction. Then the mole ratios of other steps might be taken into account:

Example:

Step 1: $2H_2O \leftrightarrows H_3O^+ + OH^-$ fast
Step 2: $1 CH_3Cl + OH^- \rightarrow CH_3OH + Cl^-$ slow

$CH_3Cl + H_2O \rightarrow CH_3OH + HCl$ (overall reaction)

Rate equation: rate = $k[CH_3Cl]^1[H_2O]^2$

The OH⁻ needed in the rate determining step is formed from two water molecules in the previous step => second order in respect to H_2O

Concentration-Time Graphs & Half-Life

Concentration-time graphs (three points & three graphs)

(Maths – two points)

Definition of half-life

Half-life constant for...

Graph to determine half-life

Equation to calculate k for 1st order reaction from half-life

Concentration-Time Graphs

- to determine order in respect to reactant A by measuring [A] over time
- keep concentrations of other reactants, e.g. [B], constant by using **excess**
- shape of graph indicates order:

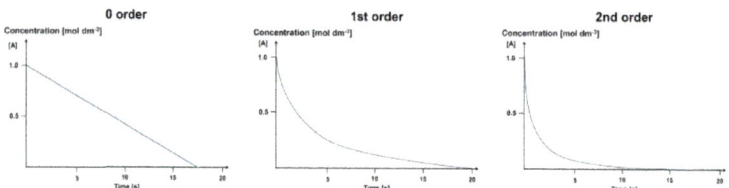

Concentration can be measured with different methods (see Year 1 revision card)
-> best if continuously measured (e.g. colorimeter)

Maths
- *For first order reactions: graph becomes a straight line if ln[A] is plotted against time (slope = -k)*
- *For second order reactions: graph becomes a straight line if 1/[A] is plotted against time (slope = k)*

Half-life $t_{1/2}$

Definition: the time required to reach half the initial concentration

Half-life constant for first order reactions:

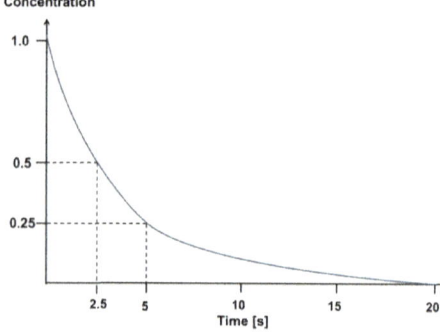

-> $t_{1/2} = 2.5$ s

Calculate k for 1st order reaction: $k = \dfrac{\ln 2}{t_{1/2}}$

Rate-Concentration Graphs

How to create rate-concentration graphs (three points)
Initial rates method
Rate-concentration graphs (three graphs and two points)
Iodine-clock

Rate-concentration graphs

- To determine order with respect to reactant (A) by varying concentration of (A) and calculating initial rate of reactant from concentration-time graphs
- For 0 order reaction: gradient of concentration-time graph equals rate
- **Initial rates method:** draw tangent through concentration at 0 s and calculate gradient to get initial rate for 1st and 2nd order reaction

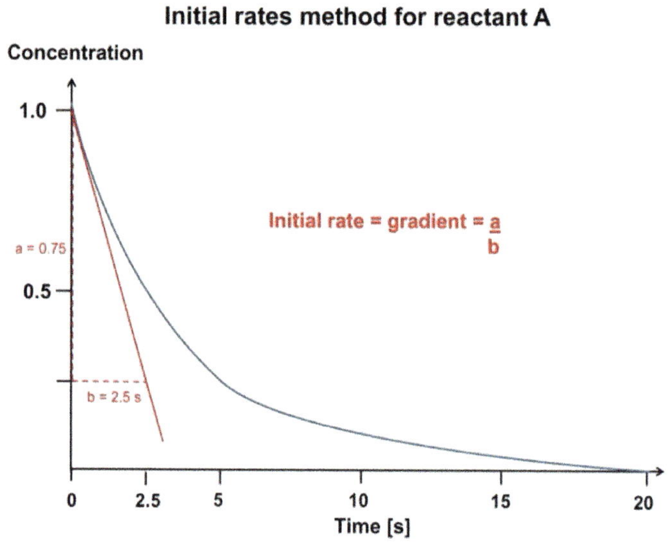

Initial rates method for reactant A

(Graph: Concentration vs Time [s], showing concentration starting at 1.0, with tangent at t=0 giving a=0.75, b=2.5 s, Initial rate = gradient = $\frac{a}{b}$)

Plot **initial rates against concentration** of A to get rate-concentration graphs for A:

Rate-concentration graphs

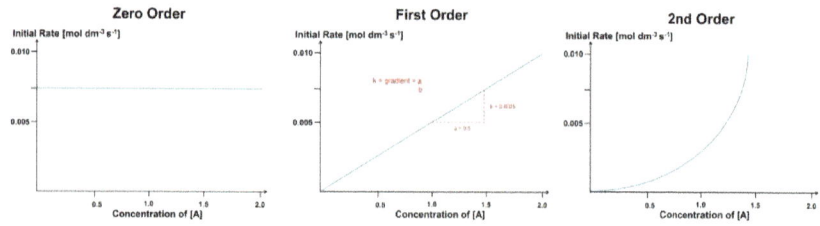

- For first order reactions: k = gradient of line
- For second order reactions: the graph becomes a straight line if plotted against (concentration)^2
- Iodine clock: Plot 1/t instead of rate to get same graphs -> much simpler experiment

Iodine Clock

Purpose

Method

Relationship between time and rate

Two Applications

Iodine clock

-> can be used to determine rate of reaction *(or activation energy E_a)*

Iodine is generated in a redox reaction **(slow reaction):**

1) $2I^- + S_2O_8^{2-} \rightarrow I_2 + 2SO_4^{2-}$
   (peroxidisulfate)

-> in the presence of starch a **dark blue** complex with I_2 would form,

but is removed immediately (fast reaction):

2) $I_2 + 2S_2O_3^{2-} \rightarrow 2I^- + S_4O_6^{2-}$
   thiosulfate   *(tetrathionate)*

-> **colour** does not appear until all of the thiosulfate $S_2O_3^{2-}$ is used up

==The time (t) it takes until colour appears is inversely proportional to the rate (or rate constant k) of reaction==
-> the faster the first reaction the shorter the time
-> this time t is measured with a stop watch and recorded
=> reaction is like a **stop watch** (therefore called 'clock')

If we change conditions (concentration/temperature) which increases the rate of the first reaction then the time until the colour appears shortens.

Applications

Rate-concentration graphs
Plot 1/t instead of rate against concentration
-> measuring the time is much simpler than to determining rate
=> leads to the same graphs

Arrhenius Plot
Plot ln 1/t instead of ln k to determine activation energy E_a
-> measuring the time is much simpler than to determining rate constant k
- see revision card 'Arrhenius Equation'

Arrhenius Equation

Purpose
Arrhenius plot (four points)
Rearranged Arrhenius equation
Equation for gradient

Arrhenius equation

is used to calculate activation energy E_a

$$k = A \, e^{-E_a/RT}$$ -> *data sheet*

- k: rate constant
- A: a constant
- **E_a: activation energy**
- R: gas constant 8.31 J K^{-1} mol^{-1} ($N_A * k_B$)   -> *data sheet*
- T: temperature in K

Arrhenius Plot
- vary temperature T and measure k (or t, see "iodine clock")
- record in a table and plot ln k (or ln 1/t) against 1/T
- determine gradient m of line: m = - E_a/R
- rearrange equation towards E_a = -(m x R)

$ln \; k = - \dfrac{E_a}{R} \dfrac{1}{T} + lnA$ -> logarithmic form of equation

$y \;\; = \;\; m * x \; + \; c$ -> equation for a linear graph

plot ln k against 1/T to determine E_a -> *straight line (descending)*

gradient $-m = \dfrac{-E_a}{R}$ -> negative gradient (-m)

=> E_a = -(-m x 8.31)

-> **E_a is always positive**

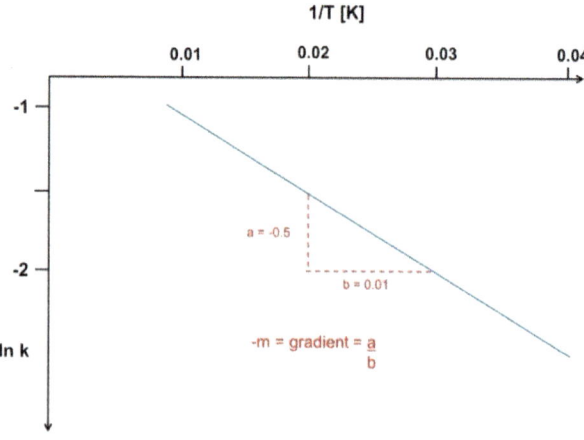

-> see also revision card 'iodine clock'

1.10 Gas Equilibrium

Gas Equilibrium

Equation for total pressure of gas mixture
Equation for mole fraction
Equation for partial pressure
Equation for Equilibrium constant K_p
Properties of K_p (two points)
Example calculation

Gas Equilibrium

==-> see Year 1 revision card 'Equilibrium and Reversible Reactions'==

The total pressure of a gas mixture is the sum of all partial pressures of the individual gases

$$p_{total} = \Sigma p_{partial}$$

p: pressure [kPa]

Partial pressures can be calculated from mole fractions:

$$\text{Mole fraction } \chi = \frac{n \text{ (one gas)}}{\Sigma n \text{ (all gases)}}$$

n: moles [mol]
χ: chi

$$p_{partial} = \chi \times p_{total}$$

Equilibrium constant K_p can be calculated from partial pressures:

$$aA_{(g)} + bB_{(g)} \rightleftharpoons cC_{(g)} + dD_{(g)}$$

$$K_p = \frac{p(C)^c \, p(D)^d}{p(A)^a p(B)^b}$$

K_p: equilibrium constant
-> ==only temperature dependent== => see Year 1 revision card
-> *liquids and solids do not appear in the equilibrium equation of a heterogeneous system*

Example

3.0 moles of PCl_5 have been thermally decomposed in a sealed container. The equilibrium mixture contains **1.75 mol** of chlorine gas. The **total pressure is 678 kPa**. Calculate the partial pressure of PCl_5.

$$PCl_5 \rightleftharpoons PCl_3 + Cl_2$$

	PCl_5	PCl_3	Cl_2
Initial moles	3.0		
Equilibrium moles	1.25	1.75	1.75

Equilibrium moles of reactant (PCl_5): ==$n_r = n_0 - x$== = 3.0 – 1.75 = 1.25

Σ n (all gases) = (1.75 moles + 1.75 moles + 1.25 moles) = **4.75 moles**

Mole fraction χ (PCl_5) = $\dfrac{1.25 \text{ moles}}{4.75 \text{ moles}}$ = **0.263**

$p_{partial}$ (PCl_5) = $\chi \times p_{total}$ = 0.263 x 678 kPa = **178 kPa**

1.11 Electrode Potentials

Electrode Potentials

Definition for standard electrode potential
Standard hydrogen half-cell with conditions (five points)
Diagram of electrochemical cell with hydrogen half-cell
Rules for electrode potential (five)
Rules for cell diagrams with example (three)

Electrode Potentials

Standard electrode potential $E^{\ominus}$

Definition: Voltage of a half-cell measured against a standard hydrogen half-cell, under standard conditions

Standard hydrogen half-cell: <mark>1M HCl, 298K, 100 kPa H_2 (Pt|H_2|H^+|| ...)</mark>
- the voltage ($E^{\ominus}$) of the standard hydrogen half-cell is **defined as 0V**
- other half-cell contains **1 M ion solution** and is connected by salt bridge
- when two ions form a half-cell (Fe^{2+}/Fe^{3+}) **platinum** is used as an **electrode**
- electrode potentials express the tendency to lose or gain electrons
- Ions move through **salt bridge** to complete circuit (maintain charge balance)

Standard hydrogen half-cell (H^+|H_2)

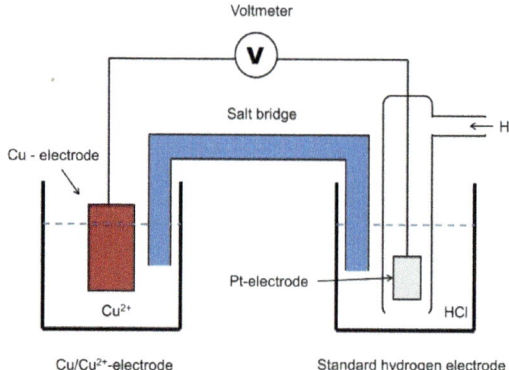

Rules for Electrode Potentials
1) **The greater the tendency of a metal to lose electrons (being oxidized) the more negative the potential**
2) Half-equations are always written as equilibrium with double arrows *(sometimes single arrows in exams/literature due to typeset limitations)*
3) By convention, half reactions of electrochemical cells are always written as a reduction process (species with more positive oxidation number first).
   $Cu^{2+} + 2e^- \rightleftharpoons Cu$
   <mark>(This does not apply to half equations of normal Redox equations)</mark>
4) Potential depends on temperature and concentration (or pressure for gases)
5) **A change of concentration or pressure (gases) which increases the number of electrons lost, makes the potential more negative**

Rules for Cell Diagrams
1. Write half-cell with the more negative potentials first
2. Oxidised forms (ions) go in the middle next to double lines (salt bridge)
3. Write inert electrodes (Pt) always on the outside
4. Example: Pt | H_2 | H^+ || Cu^{2+} | Cu

Redox Equations

How to combine half-equations (six points)
Predicting redox reactions (three points)
Example

Redox Equations

Combine half-equations to produce full (ionic) equations
- write the half equations as forward reactions (oxidation/reduction)
- use oxidation states to determine the number of transferred electrons
- **number of electrons** transferred must be the same for the full equation
- multiply both half-equations to get the lowest common multiple (here: **6**)
- **cancel** everything which appears on both sides of the equations, e.g. electrons, H^+, H_2O etc. (here: **electrons**)
- to combine to a full equation, add all remaining reactants ($2Fe^{3+}$, $3Zn$) and products ($2Fe$, $3Zn^{2+}$) together on their respective sides.

$$Fe^{3+} + 3e^- \rightarrow Fe \qquad | \times 2$$
$$Zn \rightarrow Zn^{2+} + 2e^- \qquad | \times 3$$

$$3Zn + 2Fe^{3+} \rightarrow 2Fe + 3Zn^{2+}$$
$$\;\;0 \quad\;\; +3 \qquad\;\; 0 \quad\;\; +2$$

Predicting direction of redox reaction (checking if a redox pair can react)

a) half-equation with **more negative potential** loses electrons (oxidation); **more positive potential** gains electrons (reduction)
b) highlight (**bold arrows**) the direction of the reaction according to potential and circle the **reactants** required *(example below: Zn/Zn^{2+} has lowest potential and reaction goes to the left to lose electrons, hence Ag/Ag^+ goes to the right)*.
c) see if the **reactants** are present on the left side of the overall reaction equation to decide if the pair of compounds can react

Example

Does Ag react with Zn^{2+} i.e. would the reaction $Zn^{2+} + 2Ag \rightarrow Zn + 2Ag^+$ happen?

$$Zn^{2+} + 2e^- \leftrightarrows Zn \qquad E^0 = -0.76 \text{ V}$$
$$Ag^+ + e^- \leftrightarrows Ag \qquad E^0 = +0.80 \text{ V}$$

Answer: No, because according to their potentials only **Zn** and **Ag⁺** could react (circled) and they are not the **reactants** in the overall equation.

Calculating Voltages of Cells
&
Applications of Electrochemical Cells

Equation to calculate E_{cell}

E_{cell} proportional to...

Applications of Electrochemical cells

Three cell types with properties and examples

Electrode reactions for lithium cell

Electrode reactions for alkaline hydrogen-oxygen fuel cell

Other application

Calculating voltage of electrochemical cell E_{cell} (Electromotive force: EMF)

$$E_{cell} = E_{higher\ (Red)} - E_{lower\ (Ox)}$$

-> always positive

E_{cell} proportional to ΔS_{total} and lnK

Applications of Electrochemical Cells

- The potential difference between two electrochemical half cells creates an electromotive force (EMF) in an electrochemical cell: E_{cell}
- This force is able to drive electrical devices like mobile phones & tablets

Cell types

- **Batteries – non rechargable** (irreversible reactions)
  e.g. alkaline batteries (Zn/C)
  -> cheap, last longer but create more waste
- **Storage Cells – rechargeable** (reversible reactions)
  e.g. rechargeable batteries like Lithium- or Ni/Cd cells
  -> more power, saves money over time, less waste but more toxic and expensive
- **Fuel Cells:** creates a voltage through the reaction of a fuel with oxygen
  e.g. alkaline hydrogen-oxygen fuel cells. The fuel is fed into the cell.
  -> no recharging, no toxic waste (H_2O), no direct CO_2 emission, more efficient than combustion; but H_2 is explosive, difficult to store and needs energy to produce (fossil fuel)

Lithium Storage Cell

Negative electrode (-): $Li \rightarrow Li^+ + e^-$
Positive electrode (+): $Li^+ + CoO_2 + e^- \rightarrow Li^+[CoO_2]^-$
Overall: $Li + CoO_2 \rightarrow Li^+[CoO_2]^-$

Alkaline Hydrogen-Oxygen Full Cell

Negative electrode (-): $2H_2 + 4OH^- \rightarrow 4H_2O + 4e^-$
Positive electrode (+): $2H_2O + O_2 + 4e^- \rightarrow 4OH^-$
Overall: $2H_2 + O_2 \rightarrow 2H_2O$

Other application

- **Corrosion prevention**: zinc coating for iron products prevents rusting

1.12 Acids, Bases and Buffers

Strong Acids and Bases

pH-Definition

Calculate pH of strong acid

Monoprotic and diprotic acids

Acid strength

Conjugated acid-base pairs

Ionic product of water

Equation for calculating pH of strong base

Chemical formula of hydronium ion

pH scale

Maths

Strong Acids & Bases

pH-Definition:

$$pH = -\log_{10}[H^+]$$

Calculate pH of strong acid

$$pH = -\log_{10}[H^+]$$

=> **$[H^+]$ equals concentration of the acid e.g. HCl**, unless it is a diprotic acid, like H_2SO_4, which has double the H^+ concentration

Monoprotic (monobasic):   HCl -> H^+ + Cl^-
Diprotic (dibasic): H_2SO_4 -> $2H^+$ + SO_4^{2-}

-> If the strong acid is neutralised with a strong base, subtract the moles of OH^- from the initial moles of H^+ before calculating the resulting pH

The stronger the ability of an acid to donate protons, the stronger the acid

An acid can become a base if paired with a stronger acid, forming new **conjugated acid-base pairs**:

$HNO_{3(l)}$ + $H_2SO_{4(l)}$ ⇌ $H_2NO_3^+{}_{(l)}$ + $HSO_4^-{}_{(l)}$
base1   acid2   acid1   base2

H_2SO_4/HSO_4^- are a **conjugated acid-base pair**

Ionic product of water:

$$H_2O \rightleftharpoons H^+ + OH^-$$ (slightly dissociated)

$k_w = [H^+] \times [OH^-] = 10^{-14} \, mol^2 \, dm^{-6}$

=> **increases with temperature increase (endothermic bond breaking)**

pH of strong base:

$$pH = 14 + \log[OH^-]$$

=> **$[OH^-]$ equals concentration of the base** (e.g. NaOH), unless the chemical formula of the base contains more than one mole of OH^- ions (e.g. $Ca(OH)_2$ -> double OH^- concentration)

H^+ forms H_3O^+ (hydronium ions) with water

pH scale: acidic < 7 neutral < alkaline

Maths:
$0.001 = 1 \times 10^{-3}$ -> **use standard form for scientific calculations**
$\log 1 \times 10^{-3} = -3$
$\log \sqrt{} = \frac{1}{2}$
$\log(x*y) = \log x + \log y$

Weak Acids

Equilibrium equation and equilibrium law

How to calculate the pH of a weak acid

Two assumptions

Definition of pKa

Example calculation

Weak Acids

$$HA \rightleftharpoons H^+ + A^-$$

$$K_a = \frac{[H^+][A^-]}{[HA]}$$

K_a: acid dissociation constant [mol dm^{-3}]
-> the larger K_a, the stronger the acid (more dissociation, higher [H$^+$])
[HA]: acid concentration at equilibrium [HA]$_{eq}$

Calculate pH of weak acid:

1st assumption: [A$^-$] = [H$^+$]   (neglects H$_2$O dissociation)
2nd assumption: [HA]$_{eq}$ = [HA]$_{initial}$ (neglects HA dissociation)
        -> only valid if dissociation is negligible e.g. K_a is relatively small

Rearrange equilibrium constant equation towards [H$^+$]:

$$[H^+] = \sqrt{(K_a \times [HA])}$$

$$pH = \tfrac{1}{2}(pk_a - \log[HA]) \qquad \text{(-log of the equation above)}$$

pK$_a$

$$pk_a = -\log K_a$$

the larger pk$_a$, the weaker the acid (similar to pH), e.g. chloric(I) acid HClO (pk$_a$ 7.4) weaker acid than ethanoic acid (pK$_a$ 4.8)

Example calculation

Calculate the pH of 0.001 mol dm^{-3} methanoic acid (K_a = 1.6 x 10^{-4} mol dm^{-3})

$$K_a = \frac{[H^+][A^-]}{[HA]}$$

[A$^-$] = [H$^+$]

[HA]$_{eq}$ = [HA]$_{initial}$

[H$^+$]^2 = k_a x [HA]$_{initial}$ = 1.6 x 10^{-4} mol dm^{-3} x 0.001 mol dm^{-3}
                      = 1.6 x 10^{-7} mol^2 dm^{-6}

[H$^+$] = $\sqrt{1.6 \times 10^{-7}}$ mol^2 dm^{-6} = 4 x 10^{-4} mol dm^{-3}

pH = -log [H$^+$] = -log 4 x 10^{-4} = 3.4

Buffers

General definition of buffer

Definitions for acidic and basic buffers

Two ways of buffer preparations

Workings of a buffer

pH-calculation for buffer

Tip

Applications (tree points)

Buffers

Definition: A solution that minimizes pH changes on addition of small amounts of acid or alkali.

A buffer is an aqueous mixture of a weak acid and its salt (conjugate base) in **high concentrations** -> **acidic buffer**   *or*
Mixture of weak base and its salt -> **basic buffer**

Preparations

I) Mix a weak acid and its salt ($CH_3COOH + CH_3COONa$)   *or*

II) Mix excess weak acid with a limited amount of strong alkali (NaOH)
    -> salt is formed during the neutralization reaction

Workings of a buffer

$$HA \rightleftharpoons H^+ + A^-$$

Adding H^+: system moves to the left: A^- removes H^+ by forming HA
Adding OH^-: OH^- removes H^+ by forming water; system moves to the right: **HA** dissociates replacing H^+

Calculate pH:

$$[H^+] = K_a \times \frac{[HA]}{[A^-]}$$

$$pH = pk_a + \log \frac{[A^-]}{[HA]} \qquad \textit{Henderson-Hasselbalch equation}$$

$[A^-]$: concentration of salt (base)   **Assumption:** salt fully dissociated
$[HA]$: concentration of acid   **Assumption:** $[HA]_{eq} = [HA]_{initial}$

-> **If $[HA] = [A^-]$ then $pH = pk_a$**

pH range of buffers: pk_a +/- 1

Applications

- **Biological buffer**, e.g. blood (H_2CO_3/HCO_3^-, pH 7.35 – 7.45)
- **Shampoo** (pH 5.5 -> equal to skin pH)
- **Biological washing powder** (correct pH for enzymes)

Buffer Example Calculations

Buffer Example Calculations

I) What is the pH of a buffer, after mixing **100 cm^3 0.10 mol dm^{-3}** ethanoic acid with **300 cm^3 0.20 mol dm^{-3}** sodium ethanoate?

pk$_a$ (ethanoic acid) = 4.77, K$_a$ = 1.7 x 10^{-5} mol dm^{-3}

Calculation:

Final volume: 100 cm^3 + 300 cm^3 = 400 cm^3

c (CH$_3$COOH) = (0.1 dm^{-3} x 0.1 mol dm^{-3}) / 0.4 dm^3 = 0.025 mol dm^{-3}

c (CH$_3$COONa) = (0.3 dm^{-3} x 0.2 mol dm^{-3}) / 0.4 dm^3 = 0.150 mol dm^{-3}

$$pH = pka + \log \frac{[A^-]}{[HA]}$$

$$pH = 4.77 + \log \frac{0.150}{0.025}$$

pH = 5.55

II a) What is the pH of a buffer, after mixing propanoic acid and propanoate ions with final **concentrations of 1.00 mol dm^{-3}** for both?

b) What is the pH after **6.90 g** of **Na** have been added to 1.00 dm^3 of this buffer?

K$_a$ (propanoic acid) = 1.35 x 10^{-5} mol dm^{-3}

a) pH = pka = -log 1.35 x 10^{-5}

pH = 4.87

b) Na + CH$_3$CH$_2$COOH -> CH$_3$CH$_2$COONa + H$_2$

The reaction with sodium removes some acid and produces more of the salt

n(Na) = 6.9 g / 23 g mol^{-1} = 0.30 mol

Mole ratios: Na : HA : A$^-$ 1 : 1 : 1

In 1 dm^3:

n(CH$_3$CH$_2$COOH) = 1.00 mol − (0.30 mol) = 0.7 mol   (- HA removed)

n(CH$_3$CH$_2$COO$^-$) = 1.00 mol + (0.30 mol) = 1.3 mol   (+ A$^-$ produced)

$$pH = pka + \log \frac{[A^-]}{[HA]} = 4.87 + \log \frac{1.3}{0.7}$$

pH = 4.87 + 0.269

pH = 5.14

Titration Curves I

Characteristics of titration curves (three points)
Graph strong acid/strong base
Graph weak acid/strong base (three points)
(Half-equivalence point)

Titration curves I

Titrations -> see Year 1 flashcard 'Titrations'

- **area around equivalence point has to be drawn as a straight vertical line**
- start and end point of the curve have to match the pH of the solutions used
- the pH of the indicator's colour change must match the equivalence point

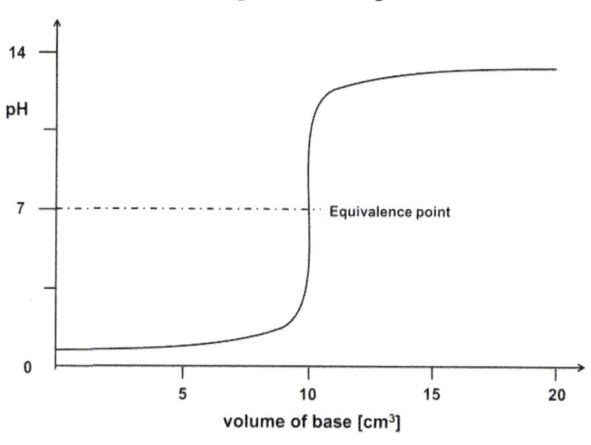

Strong Acid / Strong Base

(pH vs volume of base [cm³] graph; equivalence point at pH 7, ~10 cm³)

-> **any indicator**

Weak Acid / Strong Base

(pH vs Volume of base [cm³] graph; equivalence point above 7; half equivalence point where pH = pk_a; buffer region indicated)

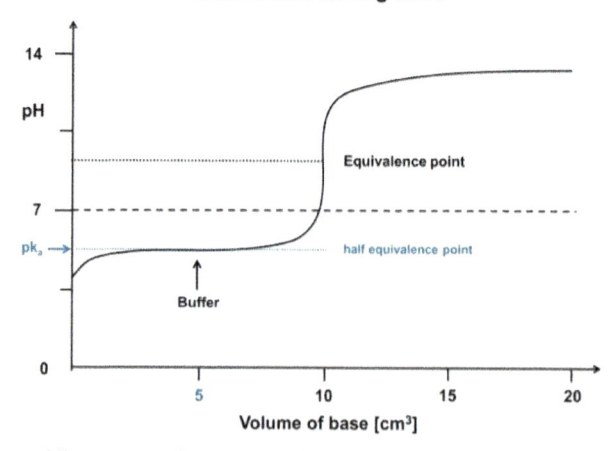

-> adding a strong base to a weak acid forms a **buffer** (see revision card)
-> *phenolphthalein (colourless -> pink) -> data sheet*
-> equivalence point above 7 because the salt produced is alkaline

Half-equivalence point: *Half of the acid has been neutralized (here at 5 cm³)*
- $pH = pk_a$ *of weak acid:* $[HA] = [A^-]$ *=> cancel out in equilibrium equation*

Titration Curves II

Graph strong acid/weak base (two points)
Graph weak acid/weak base (one point)
How to record titration curves
Difference in graph of diprotic acid

Titration curves II

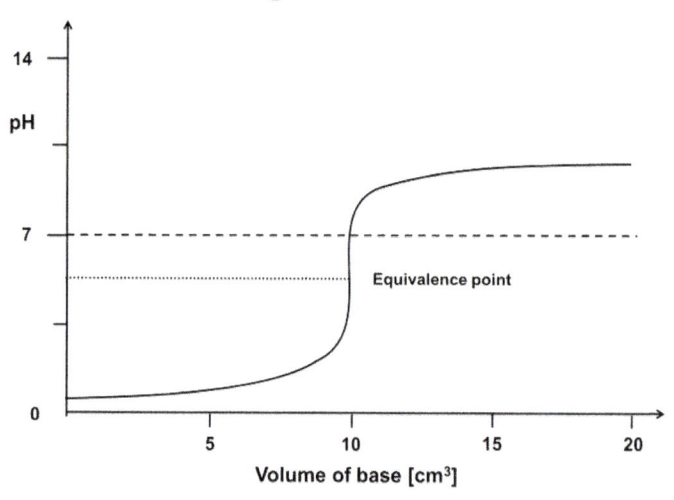

Strong Acid / Weak Base

-> *methyl orange (red -> yellow)* -> **data sheet**
-> equivalence point below 7 because the salt produced is acidic

Weak Acid / Weak Base

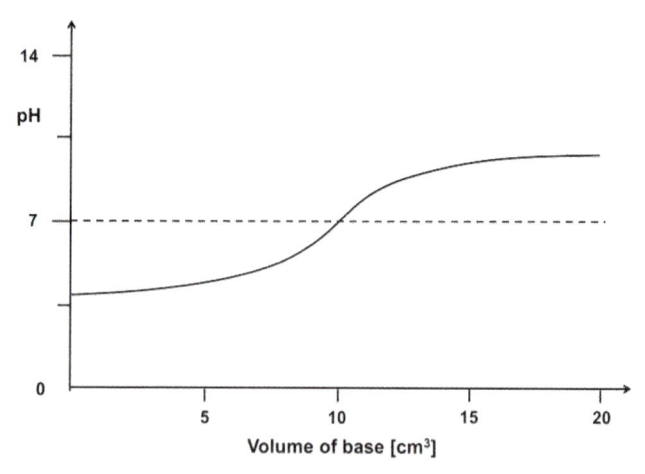

-> **Not suitable for titration with indicator (no significant pH-jump)**

- to record titration curves, increasing volumes of the standard solution are added with a burette and the pH is continuously measured with a pH meter

- weak **diprotic acids** will have two equivalence points (two stages)

Unit 2 – Inorganic Chemistry
2.4 Properties of Period 3 Elements

Properties of Period 3 Elements

Reactions of Na and Mg (four points)
Reactions of P and S with Oxygen (two equations)
Contact process (two equations)
Melting points
Reactions of Oxides with water (three equations)
Amphoteric Oxides (two equations)
Acid-base reaction (one equation)

Properties of Period 3 Elements

-> See Year 1 revision cards in Unit 2

Reactions of Na and Mg

- Na is more reactive than Mg, because Na has lower ionisation energy
- Na reacts vigorously with cold water forming a strong alkaline solution
  -> fizzing H_2; molten ball on surface, pH 12 – 14
  $$2Na_{(s)} + 2H_2O_{(l)} \rightarrow 2NaOH_{(aq)} + H_{2(g)}$$
- Mg reacts very slowly with cold water forming a weak alkaline solution
  -> pH 9- 10 (Magnesium hydroxid not very soluble in H_2O)
  $$Mg_{(s)} + 2H_2O_{(l)} \rightarrow Mg(OH)_{2(aq)} + H_{2(g)}$$
- Mg reacts fast with steam (more energy)
  $$Mg_{(s)} + H_2O_{(l)} \rightarrow MgO_{(s)} + H_{2(g)}$$

Reactions with Oxygen

$P_{4(s)} + 5O_{2(g)} \rightarrow P_4O_{10(g)}$ phosphorus(V) oxide
$S_{(s)} + O_{2(g)} \rightarrow SO_{2(g)}$ sulphur dioxide

Contact process:

$V_2O_5 + SO_2 \rightarrow V_2O_4 + \mathbf{SO_3}$
$V_2O_4 + \frac{1}{2}O_2 \rightarrow V_2O_5$ (regeneration of catalyst)

-> Al and Si are slowly oxidised, while Na, Mg and P, S react fast

Melting points

$Na_2O < MgO > Al_2O_3$ ionic lattices, but Al_2O_3 partially covalent
$> SiO_2$ giant covalent structure
$> P_4O_{10} > SO_2$ simple covalent (Dipole-Dipole & Van der Waals)

Reactions of Oxides with water

-> See Year 1 revision card 'Acids and Bases Preparation'

$P_4O_{10(s)} + 6H_2O_{(l)} \rightarrow 4H_3PO_{4(aq)}$ phosphoric acid
$SO_{2(g)} + H_2O_{(l)} \rightarrow H_2SO_{3(aq)}$ sulfurous acid, sulfuric(IV) acid
$SO_{3(g)} + H_2O_{(l)} \rightarrow H_2SO_{4(aq)}$ sulfuric acid, sulfuric(VI) acid

Amphoteric Oxides -> react as **acids** and **bases**

$Al_2O_{3(s)} + 2NaOH_{(aq)} + 3H_2O_{(l)} \rightarrow 2NaAl(OH)_{4(aq)}$
$Al_2O_{3(s)} + 6HCl \rightarrow 2AlCl_{3(aq)} + 3H_2O_{(l)}$

Acid Base Reaction

$P_4O_{10(s)} + 12 NaOH_{(aq)} \rightarrow 4Na_3PO_{4(aq)} + 6H_2O_{(l)}$

2.5 Transition Metals

Redox Titrations

General characteristics (five points)
Four reaction equations
Reaction equation for Tollens reaction
Working through a redox titration question (five points)

Redox Titration

- Can be used to determine the concentration of a substance which can be oxidized or reduced
- Needs a suitable indicator, which is difficult for Redox reactions (ideally one of the reactants/products changes colour e.g. potassium manganate (VII) purple -> pink/colourless)
- No big jump at the equivalence point as with pH titration
- The endpoint is reached, when the solution in the flask takes on the colour of the solution in the burette (unless an indicator, e.g. starch, is used)
- Often I_2/starch complex (dark blue) is used as an indicator (blue colour disappears or shows up). This might require a second redox reaction

Reactions used in redox titrations:

$MnO_4^-{}_{purple} + 8H^+ + 5e^- \rightarrow Mn^{2+}{}_{pink} + 4H_2O$
-> use diluted H_2SO_4 only: ensures complete reduction to Mn^{2+} and not MnO_2

$Fe^{2+} \rightarrow Fe^{3+} + e^-$

$C_2O_4^{2-} \rightarrow 2CO_2 + 2e^-$ (ethandioate $C_{+3} \rightarrow C_{+4}$)

$H_2O_2 \rightarrow O_2 + 2H^+ + 2e^-$ (hydrogenperoxide $O_{-1} \rightarrow O_0$)

$I_2{}_{blue} + 2e^- \rightarrow 2I^-{}_{colourless}$

Tollens (Silver Mirror)

$2[Ag(NH_3)_2]^+ + $ Aldehyde $_{(+1)} \rightarrow$ Carboxylic acid $_{(+3)} + 2Ag$ (silver) $+ 4NH_3$

Working through a Redox titration question

- Circle or highlight all data given in the exam question.
- Write the dilution ratio and molar ratios on the side of the mole equations.
- Work backwards, starting with calculating the number of moles of standard solution used in the actual redox titration from its concentration and volume.
- Use the molar ratios and dilution ratios for step by step backwards calculations, as shown in the example calculation (a-e).
- Strike through the ratios after they have been used in the calculation.

-> For general redox terms and rules see Year 1 revision cards

Example Calculation – Redox Titration

Redox Titration - Example Calculation

Q: **5.0 g** of hydrated copper(II) sulphate, **CuSO$_4$ ·XH$_2$O**, was dissolved in **50 cm^3 of water**. Iodide was added in excess and reacted with the Cu^{2+}-ions, forming iodine as described in equation (1). A **5 cm^3 portion** of the solution, with the produced iodine, was taken and titrated with **0.10 M sodium thiosulphate** solution, with starch as the indicator (equation 2). The endpoint was reached when the blue colour disappeared. The volume of thiosulphate solution used was **20 cm^3**, as measured with a burette. How many moles (X) of water of crystallisation does the hydrated copper sulphate contain?

1. Reaction: Forming I$_2$

An excess of I$^-$ solution is used to completely reduce the Cu^{2+} ions, whose concentration we want to determine. The moles of Cu^{2+} ions are directly proportional to the moles of I$_2$ produced in a 2:1 ratio.

(1) $2Cu^{2+} + 4I^- \rightarrow 2CuI + I_2$ (2:1)

2. Reaction: Titration of I$_2$ with thiosulphate standard solution (known concentration)

(2) $2S_2O_3^{2-} + I_2$ (blue) $\rightarrow 2I^-$ (colourless) $+ S_4O_6^{2-}$ (2:1)

From the volume of thiosulphate used, we can calculate the number of moles of I$_2$ and subsequently the number of moles/concentration of Cu^{2+} and water of crystallisation:

Steps

a) Calculate the number of moles of sodium thiosulphate used in the titration

   n = cV   = 0.1 mol dm^{-3} 0.02 dm^3 = 0.002 mol

b) Calculate the number of moles of Iodine molecules in the 5 cm^3 portion

   2:1 ratio: 0.002 mol / 2 = 0.001 mol

c) Calculate the number of moles of Iodine molecules in the 50 cm^3 original solution

   1:10 ratio: 10 x 0.001 mol = 0.01 mol

d) Calculate the number of moles of copper ions in 5.0 g of hydrated CuSO$_4$

   2:1 ratio: 2 x 0.01 mol = **0.02 mol**   = moles of anhydrous CuSO$_4$

e) Calculate the moles of water of crystallization (X) in hydrated copper (II) sulphate
-> see AS flashcard 'water of crystallisation'

   M$_r$ (CuSO$_4$) = 63.5 + 32 + 4x16 = 159.5 g/mol

   m = nM = 0.02 mol x 159.5 g mol^{-1} = 3.15 g CuSO$_4$ (anhydrous)

   m (H$_2$O) = 5 g – 3.15 g = 1.81 g

   n (H$_2$O) = 1.81 g / 18 g mol^{-1} = **0.1 mol**

   X = $\dfrac{0.1 \text{ mol}}{0.02 \text{ mol}}$ = **5**

The chemical formula of the hydrated copper (II) sulphate used in this experiment was
CuSO$_4$ · 5H$_2$O

Transition Elements

Definition

D-block elements which are not transition metals

Order of filling the subshells

Special electron configurations (two elements)

Where the colour comes from, including one equation

Properties of their oxidation states (four points)

Applications

Reason for their properties

Physical properties

Oxidation states of Vanadium (four)

Transition Elements

Definition: Transition elements have a partially filled d subshell in at least one ion

General Characteristics
- **Sc, Zn not transition metals**: ions of Sc (Sc^{3+}) and Zn (Zn^{2+}) do not behave like transition metals -> these ions have an empty or full d-subshell
- *Ga^{3+} behaves like a transition element (partially filled d subshell)*
- **4s removed and filled first before 3d** (4s lower energy than 3d)
- **Electron configuration Cr [Ar] $3d^5 4s^1$, Cu [Ar] $3d^{10} 4s^1$**
  -> half full and completely full d subshells are more stable
- They form **coloured** compounds:
  -> ligands split d-orbital into two energy levels
  -> e⁻ can be excited to a higher level by absorbing light:
  ΔE = hv
  ΔE: Energy difference between d-orbitals
  h: Planck constant **(data sheet)**
  v: frequency [Hz]
  -> remaining light is reflected and responsible for the colour
- *Maximum oxidation states according to group numbers (until group 7)*
- Variety of **different oxidation states** *(since there are only small differences between ionisation enthalpies in subshells; often +2 because of $4s^2$)*,
- Oxidation number is written as roman numerals, in brackets in the salt name, e.g. Iron(II) sulphate: $FeSO_4$, Iron(III) sulphate: $Fe_2(SO_4)_3$
- High oxidation state -> **oxidising agent**
- Low oxidation state -> **reducing agent**
- They are good **catalysts** because of variable oxidation states and weak surface interactions between reactant and 3d/4s electrons (Fe –> ammonia, V_2O_5 –> sulphuric acid, Ni –> hydrogenation) -> **see Y1 card 'catalyst'**
- They form **complexes** (see revision card 'complexes')
- Many of the chemical and physical properties of the transition elements are due to their **unfilled d orbitals**
- They have high melting and boiling points, high density & similar ionic radii

Oxidation states of Vanadium

VO_3^-	(+5)	white solid ($NH_4VO_3 + H^+$ -> yellow solution, see below)
VO_2^+	(+5)	yellow solution
VO^{2+}	(+4)	blue solution
V^{3+}	(+3)	green solution
V^{2+}	(+2)	violet solution

-> these successive oxidation states are achieved by adding Zn to acidic, yellow vanadium(V) solution. Zn acts as reducing agent -> Zn^{2+}

Complexes

Definition for complex

Definition for ligand

Monodentate etc.

Definition for coordination number

Shapes (five points)

Ligand exchange (three points and three equations)

Chelate effect

Test for water

Chemical formulae of complexes

Haemoglobin (three points)

Complexes

Terms

Complex: Central metal atom/ion + ligands
Ligands: form **dative covalent (coordinate) bonds to metal ion**
Monodentate, **bidentate** (Ethan-1,2-diamine; $C_2O_4^{2-}$), **multidentate** (EDTA): number of coordinate bonds from **one** ligand
Coordination number (x): number of bonds between metal and ligands

Shapes

- linear **(2)**, e.g. $[Ag(NH_3)_2]^+$ (Tollens' reagent)
- tetrahedral/square planar **(4)**
- octahedral **(6)**

-> small ligands (H_2O, NH_3) are usually 6-coordinate (octahedral)
-> large ligands (Cl^-) usually 4-coordinate (tetrahedral)

Ligand exchange/substitution

- product complex usually more stable
- polydentate complex more stable than monodentate (H_2O, Cl^-)
  -> **entropy increases** due to more product molecules => **chelate effect**
- can lead to changes in coordination number, shape and overall charge, if ligands have different sizes and charges

$[Cu(H_2O)_6]^{2+}{}_{(aq)}$ blue + $4NH_3$ ⇌ $[Cu(NH_3)_4(H_2O)_2]^{2+}$ **deep-blue** + $4H_2O$

$[Cu(H_2O)_6]^{2+}{}_{(aq)}$ blue + $4Cl^-$ -> green mixture-> $[CuCl_4]^{2-}$ yellow + $6H_2O$

$[Fe(H_2O)_6]^{3+}{}_{(aq)}$ yellow + $4Cl^-$ ⇌ $[FeCl_4]^-$ yellow + $6H_2O$

$[Co(H_2O)_6]^{2+}{}_{(aq)}$ pink + $6NH_3$ ⇌ $[Co(NH_3)_6]^{2+}$ yellow + $6H_2O$

Test for H_2O

Cobalt paper: $CoCl_4^{2-}{}_{(aq)}$ blue + $6H_2O_{(l)}$ ⇌ $[Co(H_2O)_6]^{2+}{}_{(aq)}$ pink + $4Cl^-{}_{(aq)}$

Chemical Formulae

- square brackets are used for complex-formulae (and concentrations)
- **overall charge of complex** = charge central ion + sum of charges of ligands

Haemoglobin

- a complex of Fe^{2+} with *porphyrin* and globin protein
- the sixth ligand is O_2
- CO binds more strongly than O_2 => asphyxiation (poisoning)

Stereoisomerism in Transition Metal Complexes

Optical isomerism with example (draw)
Cis-trans Isomers with three examples
Cis-platin with application (draw)

Stereoisomerism in Transition Metal Complexes

Optical Isomerism *(Enantiomers)*

Octahedral complexes with bidentate ligands form two optical isomers:
[Ni(H$_2$NCH$_2$CH$_2$NH$_2$)$_3$]$^{2+}$ (Ethan-1,2-diamine – "en")

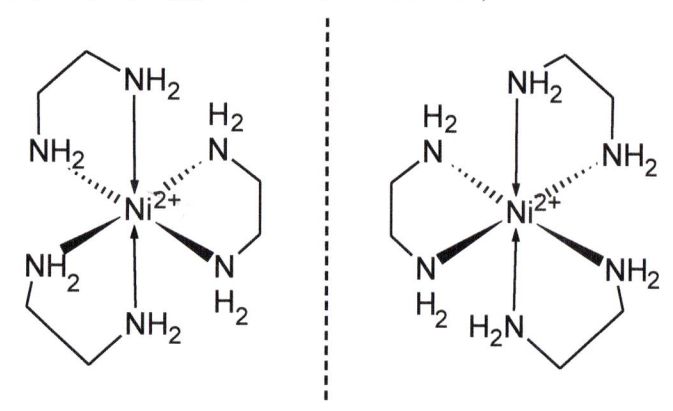

-> **need to be able to draw structures**
-> see revision card 'Optical Isomers'

Cis-trans Isomerism

Square planar and octahedral complexes with at least **two pairs of ligands** show cis/trans isomerism:

[Ni(NH$_3$)$_2$Cl$_2$]   *square planar*
[CoCl$_2$(NH$_3$)$_4$]$^+$ *octahedral*

[Pt(Cl)$_2$(NH$_3$)$_2$]   *square planar*

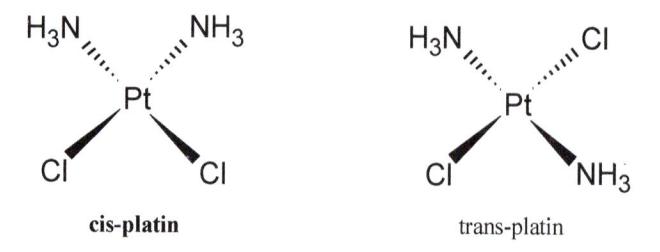

cis-platin   trans-platin

-> **cis-platin anti-cancer drug:** binds to DNA and prevents cell division

-> see Year 1 revision card 'Types of Isomers'

2.6 Reactions of Transition Metals Ions

Metal-Aqua

Reactions of Transition Metal Ions

Four Metal-aqua Complex Ions with colours
Acidity with two equations and three points
Reactions with NaOH/NH$_3$: Cu^{2+}, Fe^{2+}, Fe^{3+}, Al^{3+}
Two amphoteric reactions of Al^{3+}
Further reaction with ammonia
Two Reactions of 2+ ions with carbonate
Reaction of 3+ ions with carbonate

Reactions of Transition Metal Ions

Metal-aqua Ions

$[Cu(H_2O)_6]^{2+}$ blue
$[Fe(H_2O)_6]^{2+}$ pale green
$[Fe(H_2O)_6]^{3+}$ yellow
$[Al(H_2O)_6]^{3+}$ **colourless**

Acidity

$[M(H_2O)_6]^{2+} + H_2O \rightleftharpoons [M(H_2O)_5(OH)]^{+} + H_3O^{+}$
$[M(H_2O)_6]^{3+} + H_2O \rightleftharpoons [M(H_2O)_5(OH)]^{2+} + H_3O^{+}$

- **hydrolysis** of water
- weak **acidic** for M^{2+}
- **stronger acidic** for M^{3+} -> greater polarising power (**higher charge density**)

Test for Transition Metals

Precipitation reactions with NaOH or NH₃-solutions (release OH⁻ ions)

$Cu^{2+}_{(aq)}$ blue $+ 2OH^{-}_{(aq)}$ -> $Cu(OH)_{2(s)}$ **blue precipitate**
$Fe^{2+}_{(aq)}$ green $+ 2OH^{-}_{(aq)}$ -> $Fe(OH)_{2(s)}$ **green precipitate**
$Fe^{3+}_{(aq)}$ yellow $+ 3OH^{-}_{(aq)}$ -> $Fe(OH)_{3(s)}$ **red-brown/rust prec.**
$Al^{3+}_{(aq)}$ colourless $+ 3OH^{-}_{(aq)}$ -> $Al(OH)_{3(s)}$ **white, amphoteric:**
$Al(OH)_{3(s)}$ $+ OH^{-}_{(aq)}$ -> $[Al(OH)_4]^{-}_{(aq)}$ dissolves in excess OH⁻
$Al(H_2O)_3(OH)_{3(s)}$ $+ 3H^{+}_{(aq)}$ -> $[Al(H_2O)_6]^{3+}_{(aq)}$ dissolves in acid

-> simplified equations: use aqua-complexes instead of plain metal ions in exams

Further reaction with NH₃

$Cu(OH)_2(H_2O)_{4(s)} + 4NH_3 \rightarrow [Cu(NH_3)_4(H_2O)_2]^{2+}_{(aq)} + 2H_2O_{(l)} + 2OH^{-}_{(aq)}$
blue precipitate => **deep blue solution**

Reactions with Carbonate

$Cu^{2+}_{(aq)}$ blue $+ CO_3^{2-}_{(aq)}$ -> $CuCO_{3(s)}$ **blue/green precipitate**
$Fe^{2+}_{(aq)}$ pale green $+ CO_3^{2-}_{(aq)}$ -> $FeCO_{3(s)}$ **green precipitate**

-> M^{3+} ions form hydroxides (not carbonates) and CO_2, because of stronger acidity of 3+ ions (higher charge density) => **fizzing**

Test for other Ions
-> see Year 1 revision card 'test for ions'

Unit 3 - Organic Chemistry
3.7 Optical Isomers

Optical Isomers

Definition of optical isomers
Definition of chiral centre
Tip for chiral centre
Physical characteristics of optical isomers (one point)
Definition of racemic mixture with property
Applications (three points)

Optical Isomers

Definition
Optical Isomers (enantiomers) have a **chiral centre** and are non-superimposable **mirror images**

Chiral centre
- **Definition: Four** different atoms/groups attached to one carbon atom -> **asymmetric carbon (*)**
- Look at the entire group not just the first Carbon atom of the sidechain to decide if they are different
- *Each chiral centre doubles the number of possible optical isomers of the molecule*

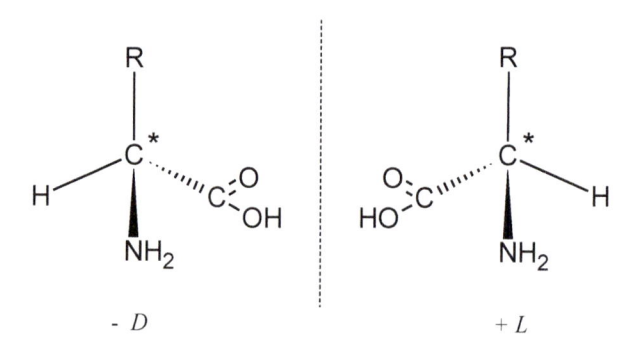

$- D$ $+ L$

Physical characteristics
- they rotate polarised light anticlockwise (−) or clockwise (+)
  => **optically active**

Racemic mixture (racemate)
- 50 : 50 mixture of both isomers
  => **not optically active**

Applications
- important for pharmaceutical drugs (thalidomide)
- amino acids
- enzymes: active sides and substrates

3.8 Aldehydes & Ketones

Aldehydes & Ketones

Naming
Properties of Carbonyl group
Mechanism of nucleophilic addition with NaBH$_4$
Mechanism of nucleophilic addition with HCN (two points)
Three tests for aldehydes/ketones

Aldehydes/Ketones

Propanone (propan-2-one)　　　Propanal

Carbonyl group　C=O
Permanent Dipole　δ+ δ-, **but not a good leaving group (double bond)**

Nucleophilic addition with NaBH₄
NaBH₄: sodium borohydride (tetrahydridoborate) in water => H⁻ (hydride)
　　　=> reduces aldehydes and ketones to primary and secondary alcohols

hydride (nucleophile)　　　secondary alcohol
R-CHO + 2[H] -> R-CH₂OH　　　[H]: reducing unit (donating 1e⁻)

Nucleophilic addition with HCN (hydrogen cyanide) to form hydroxynitriles

cyanide (nucleophile, **toxic!**)　　　**hydroxynitrile**

-> CN⁻ can attack planar carbonyl group from both sides -> **racemate**
-> KCN/H₂SO₄ preferred to HCN (weak acid), because of higher amount of CN⁻

Tests to distinguish between Aldehydes and Ketones

Tollens: test for aldehydes (AgNO₃/ammonia, test tube in warm water bath)
　2[Ag(NH₃)₂]⁺ + Aldehyde ₍₊₁₎ + 3OH⁻ -> 2**Ag** + Carb. acid ₍₊₃₎ + 2H₂O
　Aldehyde is oxidised, silver ions reduced -> silver **mirror** (not with ketone)

Fehling: test for aldehydes (Cu²⁺/NaOH₍aq₎, gentle heating)
2Cu²⁺ blue + Aldehyde -> 2Cu⁺ + Carboxylic acid (**Cu₂O** precipitate - **brick red**)

Acidified potassium dichromate -> see Y1 revision card 'Alcohols'

3.9 Carboxylic Acids and Esters

Carboxylic Acids & Anhydrides

Naming of homologous series
Properties of the functional group
Characteristics of carboxylic acids (five points)
Acid-base reaction with equation
Three tests
Preparation
Organic reaction

Equation for anhydrides-reaction with alcohols (three points)

Carboxylic acids

Homologous Series: Methanoic acid, ethanoic acid, propanoic acid,...

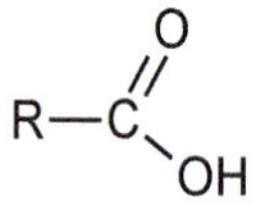

$$R-C(=O)-OH$$

Carboxyl group: strong dipole -> more polar than alcohols or aldehydes/ketones

Characteristics

- High boiling points (H-bonds)
- Boiling points increase with chain length (Van der Waals)
- Solubility decreases with chain length *(more hydrophobic)*
- IR: show a broad absorption band of OH group at 2500- 3000 cm^{-1}
- **They are weak Acids**:

Acid-base reaction

CH_3COOH + CuO (base) -> $(CH_3COO)_2Cu$ (salt – copperethano**ate**) + H_2O

Tests
- **pH-Indicator**
- R-COOH + **carbonate** -> salt + water + $CO_{2(g)}$ **fizzing, carbonate disappears**
- R-COOH + metal -> salt (carboxylate) + $H_{2(g)}$ **fizzing**, metal **disappears**

Preparation
- Oxidation of primary alcohols or aldehydes

Organic Reaction
- They form **Esters** with alcohols (see revision card 'Esters')

Acid anhydrides

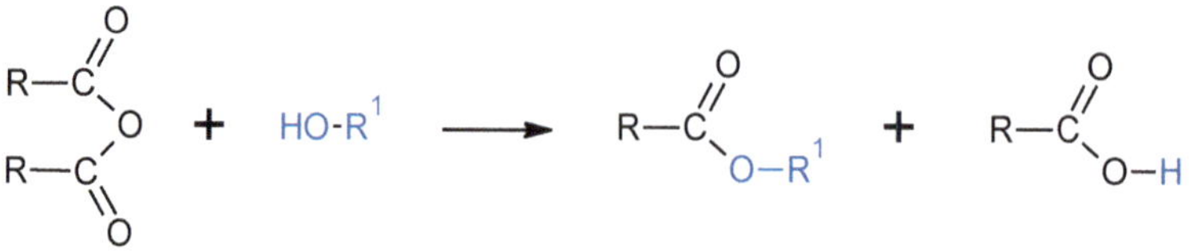

$$R-C(=O)-O-C(=O)-R + HO-R^1 \longrightarrow R-C(=O)-O-R^1 + R-C(=O)-O-H$$

Acid anhydride + alcohol   ->   ester + carboxylic acid

- no catalyst required (more reactive)
- they are hidden carboxylic acids (add water -> carboxylic acid)
- formed by a condensation reaction and split apart in a hydrolysis reaction

Esters

Esterification reaction equation

Naming of esters

Conditions, properties and type of reaction (three points)

Esterification with acid anhydride

Physical characteristics of esters (five points)

Applications (three points)

IR

Ester hydrolysis with two different reactants

Fats/oils

Esters

Esterification

$$H_3C-\underset{OH}{\overset{O}{C}} + HO-CH_3 \underset{}{\overset{H_2SO_4 \text{ conc}}{\rightleftharpoons}} H_3C-\underset{O-CH_3}{\overset{O}{C}} + H_2O$$

carboxylic acid + alcohol ⇌ Ester + water
ethanoic acid + methanol   methylethanoate

- **Conditions:** Reflux, catalyst: concentrated sulfuric acid
- Reversible reaction, equilibrium (low yield)
- Condensation, Nucleophilic Addition-Elimination reaction
- *Substitution of H of carboxylic acid with -R from alcohol*

Acid anhydride

Acid anhydride + alcohol => ester + carboxylic acid
-> No catalyst required (more reactive) => see previous revision card

Physical characteristics of esters
- Nice smell
- Neutral (no acid reactions)
- Low boiling point (no hydrogen bonds)
- Functional group isomers of carboxylic acids
- Less polar than carboxylic acids

Applications
- Perfumes & flavouring *(peach, pineapple, raspberry)*
- Biodiesel (mixture of **methyl esters** of long-chain carboxylic acids)
- Polar solvents & plasticisers

IR

Esters do not show the broad absorption band of carboxylic acids at 2500 – 3000 cm^{-1} (OH-group)

Ester hydrolysis

hot diluted H$_2$SO$_4$: $CH_3COOCH_3 + H_2O \rightleftharpoons CH_3COOH + CH_3OH$
           carboxylic acid

hot aqueous NaOH: $CH_3COOCH_3 + NaOH \rightarrow CH_3COONa + CH_3OH$
           sodium **carboxylate (ethanoate)**
-> **soap** (salts of long-chain carboxylic acids from fats)

Fats/Oils

Natural esters of propane-1,2,3-triol with fatty acids -> see next revision card

Fats & Oils

Fatty acids (six points)

Fats with two structural formulae (four points)

Saponification reaction

Acid hydrolysis

Equation for biodiesel preparation

Fats & Oils

Fatty acids

- long chain carboxylic acids
- minimum 4C (butanonic acid) -> usually at least 8C (octanoic acid)
- even number of carbon atoms
- aliphatic (non-aromatic), unbranched,
- saturated (tightly packed, higher melting point, stronger Van der Waals, animal)
- unsaturated (more space, lower melting point, healthier, vegetable, fish)

Fats

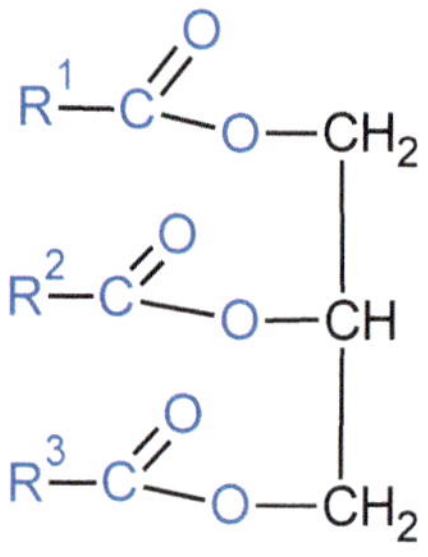

$$R^1-C(=O)-O-CH_2$$
$$R^2-C(=O)-O-CH$$
$$R^3-C(=O)-O-CH_2$$

fat

$$HO-CH_2$$
$$HO-CH$$
$$HO-CH_2$$

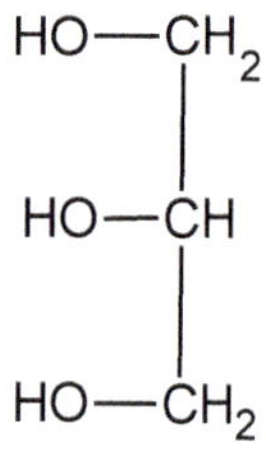

glycerol

- **Triester** (Triglyceride) of **fatty acids** and **glycerol** (**propane-1,2,3-triol**)
- Energy reserve
- Biological membranes (phospholipids, cholesterol)
- Manufacture of margarine from unsaturated vegetable oil

Saponification

Ester hydrolysis of fat with NaOH produces **salt of fatty acid (soap)** + Glycerol

    ester + base   -> salt (carboxylate)   + alcohol

Acid hydrolysis

    ester + diluted acid   -> fatty acid   + alcohol

Biodiesel

-> from vegetable oils with KOH as catalyst

    triester + methanol   -> **methyl ester**   + glycerol

Acyl Chlorides

Characteristics of functional group (three points)
Four acylation reactions with equations
Mechanism with water
Numbering of carbon atoms
Aspirin

Acylchlorides

$$H_3C-C\overset{\delta+}{\underset{Cl\;\delta-}{\overset{O\;\delta-}{\|}}}$$

Eth**anoyl chloride**

Acyl-group: highly reactive C (high δ+ charge -> strongly attracts nucleophiles)
=> **nucleophilic addition-elimination** reaction
=> Cl good leaving group; gets substituted

Acylation reactions

RCOCl + H₂O -> R−C(=O)OH + HCl   **Carboxylic acid**

R¹COCl + CH₃OH -> R¹−C(=O)O−R² + HCl   **Ester** (R²: CH₃)

RCOCl + NH₃conc -> R−C(=O)NH₂ + HCl   **Primary Amide**

R¹COCl + CH₃NH₂ -> R¹−C(=O)NH−R² + HCl   **Sec. Amide** (R²: CH₃)

-> **similar reactions and products for acid anhydrides (safer, less corrosive)**

Mechanism

H₃C−C(δ+)(=O δ−)(Cl δ−) + :Ö−H (H δ+) [**nucleophile**] → H₃C−C(−Ö⁻)(−O⁺H−H)(−Cl) → H₃C−C(=O)OH + HCl

Numbering of Carbon atoms

- Starts with the carbon of the acyl-group => 1
- Similar to numbering in carboxylic acids

Aspirin: Ester made from salicylic acid and ethanoic anhydride

3.10 Aromatic Compounds

Benzene & Arenes

Characteristics of benzene (three points)

Draw p-orbitals and electron clouds (two drawings)

Evidence for delocalised structure (three points)

Naming

Reaction type of arenes

Draw mechanism

Tip

Benzene

Characteristics
- p-orbitals of π-bonds overlap
- π-electrons **delocalised** (cannot polarise halogens like alkenes do; symbolised by the ring in the structural formula)
- **high electron densities** (electron clouds) above and below ring

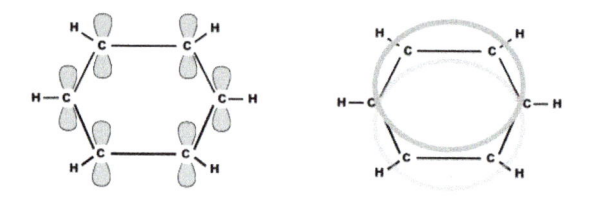

Evidence for delocalised structure
- C-C-bonds have same length (Kekulé: different lengths for single and double bonds)
- does not decolourise bromine water
- hydrogenation enthalpy less exothermic than expected (compared to 3x cyclohexene)

Naming
- 1-chloro-4-methylbenzene (alphabetic, smallest number)
- Name if side group: Phenyl C_6H_5- *(not Benzyl $C_6H_5CH_2$-)*

Arenes –aromatic compounds

Reactions: electrophilic substitutions
—> to keep delocalised system (low energy) *(Alkenes – Addition)*

Mechanism:

Benzene   + E^+ —>   E-benzene   + H^+

E^+: **Electrophile**

—> First curly arrow must touch or cross the inside ring

Reactions of Arenes

Nitration with three equations and conditions (three points)

Acylation reaction with two equations and conditions

(Alkylation)

(Halogenation)

Hydrogenation

Reactions of Arenes (Electrophilic Substitution)

Nitration with nitric acid

$H_2SO_4 + HNO_3 \rightarrow HSO_4^- + NO_2^+ + H_2O$
                nitronium ion *(nitryl cation)* -> **electrophile**

$H^+ + HSO_4^- \rightarrow H_2SO_4$ -> regeneration of catalyst

$C_6H_6 + HNO_3 \rightarrow C_6H_5NO_2 + H_2O$
                    nitrobenzene

- -> Concentrated HNO_3, sulphuric acid catalyst, below 55° C (mononitration)
- -> Reduction of nitrobenzene to aminobenzene for dyes -> see 'Amines'
- -> Explosives like TNT (**T**ri**N**itro**T**oluene)

Acylation (Friedel Crafts) with acylchloride (ethanoyl chloride)

$CH_3COCl + AlCl_3 \rightarrow CH_3CO^+ (AlCl_4)^-$

$C_6H_6 + RCO^+ \rightarrow C_6H_5COR + H^+$
                        phenyl**ketone**

> anhydrous (dry ether) **AlCl₃** (catalyst – **halogen carrier**), heat under reflux

Alkylation (Friedel Crafts)

$CH_3CH_2Cl + AlCl_3 \rightarrow CH_3CH_2^+ (AlCl_4)^-$ R^+ *(alkyl)*

$C_6H_6 + CH_3CH_2^+ \rightarrow C_6H_5CH_2CH_3 + H^+$ *(ethyl**benzene**)*
benzene + R^+ -> benzene-R   *(alkyl**benzene**)*

-> anhydrous $AlCl_3$, heat under reflux

Halogenations (Chlorination)

Halogen carriers: AlCl₃ or FeCl₃ needed as a catalyst to form X^+ ions

$AlCl_3 + Cl_2 \rightarrow AlCl_4^-$ *(dative)* $+ Cl^+ (E^+)$ *(heterolytic fission)*
$AlCl_4^- + H^+ \rightarrow AlCl_3 + HCl$ -> regeneration of catalyst

$C_6H_6 + Cl_2 \rightarrow C_6H_5Cl + HCl$
                      1-**chloro**benzene (phenylchloride)

-> RT (room temperature), dark, anhydrous

Hydrogenation (Addition)

$C_6H_6 + 3H_2 \rightarrow C_6H_{12}$
                      cyclohexane

-> *Ni-catalyst, 150° C, 10 atm*

3.11 Amines

Amines

Types of amines

Naming

Four reactions of amines with one mechanism

Application

Amines

primary R-NH₂, secondary R₂NH, tertiary R₃N, quaternary R₄N⁺
                                                    ammonium salt

Naming
$CH_3CH_2NH_2$:   1-Ethylamine, 1-aminoethan   -> aliphatic amine
$C_6H_5-NH_2$:   phenylamine (aminobenzene)   -> aromatic amine

Lone pair of electrons on <mark>nitrogen</mark> causes reactions as:

I) Bases
$CH_3CH_2NH_2 + HCl \rightarrow CH_3CH_2NH_3Cl$ $(CH_3CH_2NH_3^+ + Cl^-)$
Ethylamine   ethylammonium chloride (salt)

    aliphatic amine -> stronger bases than ammonia *(+ inductive Effect)*
    aromatic amine -> weaker bases (lone pair delocalises into the ring)

II) Alkalis (weak): $CH_3CH_2NH_2 + H_2O \rightarrow CH_3CH_2NH_3^+ + $ **OH⁻**

III) Ligands
   -> see revision card 'complexes'

IV) Nucleophiles

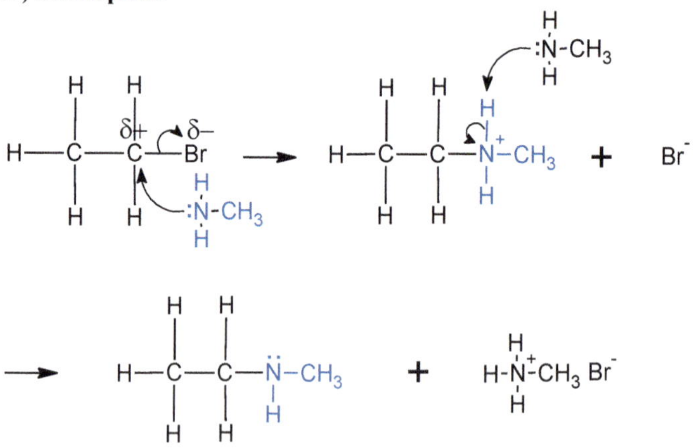

bromoalkane + **prim amine** -> **sec amine** + alkylammonium bromide
-> **nucleophilic substitution** *(second attack as base)*
-> see also revision card 'Acyl chlorides'

Application
Quaternary ammonium salts are used as cationic surfactants
-> detergent, hair conditioner

Preparation of Amines & Amides

Two methods for preparation of aliphatic amines with conditions
Naming Nitriles
Preparation of aromatic amines with conditions and application
Two methods for preparation of amides
Naming amides

Preparation of Amines

I) Aliphatic Amines from Haloalkane (Nucleophilic Substitution)

$R-X + 2NH_3 \rightarrow R-NH_2 + NH_4X$

Conditions: heat in a sealed flask with excess ammonia in ethanol
With excess RX: continues to substitute H with R until R_4N^+ (quaternary ammonium) formed
-> mixture of primary, secondary, tertiary and quaternary amines, which can be separated by fractional distillation

II) Aliphatic Amines from Nitriles (Reduction)

$R-CN + 4[H] \rightarrow R-CH_2NH_2$
nitrile   amine

Conditions:
- Ni/H_2, high temperature & pressure (catalytic hydrogenation, industry)
- $LiAlH_4$ in dry ether followed by dilute acid (expensive, lab)

-> for preparation of nitriles see Year 1 revision card 'Haloalkanes'

Naming Nitriles: $CH_3CH(CH_3)CH_2CN$ 3-Methylbutanenitrile

Aromatic Amines from Nitro compound (Reduction)

$C_6H_5NO_2 + 6[H] \rightarrow C_6H_5NH_2 + 2H_2O$

-> Reflux, Sn/HCl_{conc} -> **Reduction** with H_2; then $NaOH_{(aq)}$
-> **phenylamine** is used for formation of **Azo dyes**

Preparation of Amides (Nucleophilic Addition Elimination)

From Acylchlorides

$RCOCl + NH_3 \rightarrow RCONH_2 + HCl (NH_4Cl)$ Primary Amide

-> see revision card 'Acyl Chlorides'

From Acid anhydrides

$RC(O)OC(O)R' + 2NH_3 \rightarrow RCONH_2 + R'COONH_4$
                               primary amide + salt

-> see revision card 'Carboxylic Acids & Anhydrides'

Naming Amides: $CH_3CONHCH_3$ N-methylethanamide

3.12 Condensation Polymers

Condensation Polymers

Condensation polymerization (two points)
Polyamide preparation with two equations
Circling method
Polyester preparation with two equations
Definition of Diol
Drawing lines method
Both functional groups on same molecule
How to recognise an addition polymer

Condensation Polymers

Condensation polymerization
- **Monomers form a polymer and another small molecule (H_2O)**
- Monomers must have two functional groups

Polyamide
dicarboxylic acid + diamine -> poly-amide + water

Propane-1,3-dicarboxylic acid + 1,2 diamino-ethane

=> Circle atoms which form the water. The leftover half-bonds form the amide bonds

Polyester
dicarboxylic (dioic) acid + diol -> poly-ester + water

Propane-1,3-dicarboxylic (dioic) acid + ethan-1,2-diol

Diol: compound with two alcohol (-OH) groups

To determine monomers from a chain:
draw lines through the middle of the ester bonds and add water (OH, H) to CO and O respectively (hydrolysis).

Carboxylic acid and alcohol group on same molecule -> poly-ester + water

-> acyl chlorides can be used instead of carboxylic acids

If the polymer chain (repeat unit) is not connected by amide or ester groups, but C-C single bonds, then it is an addition polymer

-> See also Year 1 revision card 'Polymers' for addition polymers

Important Polymers

Two important polyamides
Important polyester
Biodegradable and non-biodegradable polymers
Three methods of disposal with advantage/disadvantage

Important Polymers

-> see Year 1 revision card 'Polymers'

Important Polyamides
Nylon 6,6
  -> called 6,6 because 6 Cs in both monomers
  Hexane-1,6-dicarboxylic acid + hexamethylene diamine
  $HOOC-(CH_2)_4-COOH + H_2N-(CH_2)_6-NH_2$ -> nylon + H_2O
  - elastic Fibers
  - intermolecular forces (hydrogen bonds) hold chains together

Kevlar
  Benzene-1,4-diamine + benzene-1,4-dicarboxylic acid
  - bullet-proof vests, sports equipment
  - multiple hydrogen bonds, perfectly aligned chains => very strong

Important Polyesters
Terylene (PET)
  Benzene-1,4-dicarboxylic acid + Ethane-1,2-diol
  - fibres, bottles
  - permanent dipoles & hydrogen bonds hold chains together

==Polyester and Polyamides are biodegradable==
-> can be broken down by **hydrolysis** due to polar bonds

Polyalkenes are non-biodegradable
-> non-polar bonds are chemically inert (do not react)

Disposal
- **Landfill**
  + good for biodegradable plastic, cheap
  - uses up land and pollutes surroundings
- **Incineration**
  + produces energy
  - releases toxins (most filtered out) and CO_2
- **Recycling**
  + saves resources
  - expensive separation

3.13 Amino Acids, Proteins and DNA

Amino Acids & Proteins

Definition of amino acids
Optical isomers
Definition of amphoteric
Draw structural formulae at different pH
Definition of zwitterion
Definition of isoelectric point
Building blocks of...
Protein structures
Definition of enzymes
Definition of inhibitor
Ester formation
Naming
Peptide formation with equation and reaction type
Two methods of peptide hydrolysis with equations

Amino acids

Def.: alpha-amino-carboxylic acids (NH_2 and $COOH$ attached to same Carbon *)

Optical isomers: chiral centre * -> 4 different groups at alpha C (except glycine)

Amphoteric: react as acid & base *(bifunctional molecule)* -> weak buffer

acidic (*protonated*)   intermediate pH (**zwitterion**)   alkaline (*deprotonated*)

Zwitterion: has positive and negative charges at intermediate pH
-> ionic bonds, high melting points (stronger than H-bonds) => solid salts

Isoelectric point: Intermediate pH at which amino acid has the same numbers of negative & positive charges (no overall charge)

Building blocks of Proteins (Polypeptides)
Primary (sequence), secondary (α-helix, β-sheets), tertiary (3D) structure
Intermolecular forces: salt bridges – polar interaction, van der Waals
Hydrogen bonds & covalent bonds (disulfide) -> 3D (denatured by heat & pH)
Enzymes -> biological catalysts: active sites are stereospecific (drug target)
Inhibitor: molecule which blocks active site (shape similar to substrate)

Carboxylic acid group: Ester-formation (cyclic ester with internal OH-group)

Naming: 2-aminopropanoic acid (alanine)

Peptide Formation

Alanine   Glycine   Dipeptide (AlaGly) (Amide) + water
-> condensation

=> circle atoms which form the water, then connect the leftover half-bonds to form a peptide bond

Peptide Hydrolysis

with acid: 6 M HCl, reflux heat; then neutralize
Peptide + H_2O (H^+) => protonated amino acids (+)

with alkaline: $NaOH_{conc}$
Peptide + OH^- => deprotonated amino acids (-) (carboxylate-salt)

DNA
&
Tests for Functional Groups

DNA stands for...

Building blocks of DNA

Type of polymer

Formation of the double helix

Base pair combinations

Coding

Cis-platin (five points)

Tests for five functional groups:
alkenes, haloalkanes, aldehydes, alcohols, carboxylic acids

DNA

- **D**eoxyribo**N**ucleic **A**cid
- DNA consists of **nucleotides** made up from sugar, phosphate and four different bases: adenine (A), thymine (T), cytosine (C), and guanine (G) -> *data sheet*
- The sugar is the pentose: **2-deoxyribose** -> *data sheet*
- The nucleotides (monomers) form a covalently bound condensation polymer (phosphodiester)
  -> single strand of DNA
- Two complementary strands are combined to a double helix
- The two strands are hold together by hydrogen bonds between complementary base pairs:
  A-T two hydrogen bonds
  C-G three hydrogen bonds
- Three bases codons code for one amino acid (e.g. GCT -> Alanine)
- Sequence of bases determines sequence of amino acids in proteins
- Therefore DNA contains all the genetic information of an organism

Cis-platin

- for structure see revision card 'Stereoisomerism in Transition Metal Complexes'
- anti-cancer drug which prevents cell division
- binds to DNA by forming a bond to a nitrogen atom of guanine
  -> Cl⁻ ions are displaced by N from the guanine (ligand replacement)
- also binds to healthy DNA, which leads to side effects (hair loss)
- society needs to assess the balance between benefits and adverse effects of medicines

Tests for Functional Groups

Alkenes: decolourisation of bromine -> Y1 revision card 'Alkenes'

Haloalkanes: precipitation reaction with silver nitrate -> Y1 revision card

Aldehydes: silver mirror with Tollen's reagent -> Y2 revision card

Alcohols: colour change of acidified $K_2Cr_2O_7$ -> Y1 revision card

Carboxylic acids: fizzing with carbonates -> Y2 revision card

3.14 Organic Synthesis

Preparation and Purification of Organic Compounds

Apparatus used for preparation
Four purification methods
Tests for purity (three points)

Preparation and Purification of Organic Compounds

Preparation

Reflux apparatus
- To heat a reaction mixture safely
- Electrical heaters (heating mantel) are used to avoid naked flames which could ignite flammable organic compounds
-> See Year 1 revision card 'Reflux Apparatus' for details

Purification
The products of a reaction are often contaminated with side-products or unreacted reactants. The following methods are applied to remove these:

I) Washing
- A solid product can be washed with water or an organic solvent by filtration under reduced pressure (**Büchner flask**)
- Acids can be removed by reaction with $NaHCO_3$: water and CO_2 are formed. The water insoluble organic product can be separated by using a **separating funnel** (see Year 1 revision card)

II) Drying
- Traces of water can be removed by adding anhydrous salts ($CaCl_2$, $MgSO_4$)
-> See Year 1 revision card 'Drying with Anhydrous Salts'

III) Recrystallisation
-> Removes small amounts of impurities from a compound, which is very soluble at high temperatures and insoluble at low temperatures
Method
- Hot solvent is added to the impure solid until it just dissolves -> saturated
- The solution is slowly cooled down until crystals of the product are formed
- The impurities remain in the solution, due to their lower concentration
- The pure product crystals are filtered, washed with cold solvent and dried

IV) Distillation
- The product can be separated from impurities according to their different boiling points
-> See Year 1 revision card 'Distillation Apparatus'

Tests for Purity
- A pure substance has a specific melting and boiling point, which can be compared to literature values (impurities lower melting point)
- **Measuring the melting point:** the solid is slowly heated in a capillary tube, in a beaker of oil containing a thermometer; the temperature is read when the solid melts
- **Measuring the boiling point:** use a distillation apparatus

3.15 NMR

NMR Spectroscopy: H-NMR & Carbon 13-NMR

Method

X- and y-axis of NMR spectrum

Four characteristics of H-NMR spectrum

Solvent

Converting ppm into %

Three reasons for use of TMS

Two Applications

Carbon 13-NMR (three points)

NMR spectroscopy

Method: Radio waves of a specific frequency (resonance frequency) are absorbed by the nucleus of an atom. This reverses the spin of the nucleus inside a **strong magnetic field**. (Nucleus must have odd number of nucleons)

Proton H-NMR (nuclear magnetic resonance)

NMR spectrum
Absorption (y) of electromagnetic waves against chemical shift δ (x)
-> gives information about number and position of H-atoms in a molecule:

- **Number of peaks**: number of **different H environments (types)**
- **Position of peak**: **functional group** (different shielding)
  Chemical shift δ: resonance frequency of functional group in **ppm** relative to **TMS** (internal standard, **t**e**tra**methylsilane Si(CH$_3$)$_4$)
  ppm: parts per million -> a percentage
- **Number above peak: number of protons (H)** of same type
  -> from **integration ratio / relative peak area / relative intensity / integration trace (use ruler)**
- **Spin-spin coupling:** main peak splits off into smaller peaks **(n+1)**
  -> doublet, triplet, quartet etc.
  -> indicates **number of neighbouring H: n**
  -> **H have to be bound to adjacent Carbons**
  -> only visible in high resolution NMR
  -> *H of OH does not affect C-H of neighbour*
  => *alcohol OH just one singlet peak due to H-bonding*

Solvent: CDCl$_3$ *(deuterated chloroform)* or **CCl$_4$** (H free to prevent interference)

Converting ppm into percentage: % = ppm / 10,000

Reasons for use of TMS
- gives just one, strong signal away from others
- non-toxic and inert
- low boiling point -> easy to remove from sample

Applications

MRS/MRI: Magnetic resonance scanning/imaging with low energy electromagnetic waves (radio waves) in medicine
Chemistry: helps to determine the structure of an unknown compound

Carbon 13–NMR

- number of peaks indicates number of different carbons
- chemical shift -> chemical environment of carbon (functional group)
- for arenes look at line of symmetry

How to predict NMR Spectrum from Structural Formula

Five Steps

Example butanone

Two common peaks

How to predict H-NMR spectrum from structural formula

- **Circle** the same types of hydrogens in the structural formula to get the number of peaks
- Count the number of hydrogens inside the circle. This is the number of hydrogens for that peak (peak area) => write number on top of the circle
- Count how many hydrogens are attached to adjacent carbons (n) to get the splitting pattern (n+1 -> doublet, triplet etc.) => write on top of the circle
- Identify the functional group the hydrogens belong to and get chemical shift from the table *(data sheet)* => write below the circle
- Compare this data to actual H-NMR spectra given

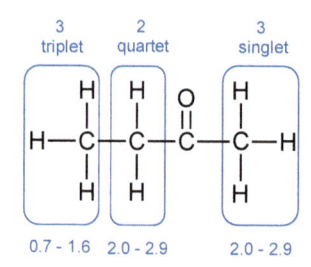

```
        3           2              3
      triplet     quartet        singlet
       ┌─┐         ┌─┐            ┌─┐
       │H│         │H│   O        │H│
       │ │         │ │   ║        │ │
   H───C───────────C───────C──────C───H
       │ │         │ │            │ │
       │H│         │H│            │H│
       └─┘         └─┘            └─┘
      0.7 - 1.6   2.0 - 2.9      2.0 - 2.9
```

=> three peaks: 3H triplet   at 1.0 ppm,
                  2H quartet   at 2.5 ppm
                  3H singlet   at 2.3 ppm

Common peaks

A) One peak with peak area 6 ($\delta = 0.8 - 2.0$)   *isopropyl*

Splitting pattern: doublet

B) Two peaks with peak areas 2 and 3 ($\delta = 0.8 - 2.0$)   **ethyl**

Splitting patterns: **2** -> quartet, quintet or sextet; **3** -> triplet

3.16 Chromatography

Thin Layer Chromatography

Purpose of chromatography

Two reasons for separation

Application

TLC steps:

Stationary and mobile phase

Method

Treatment of colourless compounds

How to measure R_f value

Standard method for...

Equation for R_f value

Chromatography

-> Separating and identifying components of a mixture (**solutes**) by degree of interaction with the stationary phase (temperature dependent):

- Separation due to different **adsorption** to matrix **(solid)** -> **TLC, GC**
- or different **solubility (liquid)** -> **GLC, CC (TLC)**

Application: Quality control in industry (purity & identity)

Thin Layer Chromatography (TLC)

- Stationary phase (solid matrix): silica (SiO_2) or alumina (Al_2O_3) coated glass/plastic plate
- Mobile phase: liquid (alcohol, ester)
- Spots of the mixture and reference substances are put on a pencil line at the lower edge of the plate (starting point)
- The plate is placed in a beaker with liquid below the pencil line
- The liquid travels up the plate by capillary forces taking the compounds with it
- The components travel at different speeds due to different adsorption
- The plate is taken out when sufficient separation is achieved (end point)
- Mark the position of the solvent front with a pencil
- Colourless compounds (**amino acids**) have to be treated with ninhydrin, iodine or UV light to make them visible on the dried plate
- Measure distance from starting pencil line to the spot (a) and the solvent front line (x)
- Compare R_f value of the unknown component with that of the known/pure compound (reference)
- Standard method to separate and **identify amino acids** after hydrolysis of **proteins**

R_f value:

$$R_f = \frac{a}{x}$$

- a: distance moved by solute (compound) in cm
- x: distance moved by solvent in cm
- R_f: **Retardation Factor (retention factor)**

Gas Chromatography
&
Column Chromatography

Three parts of the GLC Apparatus

Chromatogram (two points with equation)

Definition of retention time

Limitations (three points)

Applications (two points)

Column Chromatography:

Application

Stationary and mobile phase

Method (four points)

Gas Liquid Chromatography GLC (GC)

Apparatus
- **Inlet:** injection of liquid (heated to vaporize) or gas sample (not heated)
- **Column:**
  - filled with viscous liquid (GLC) or solid (GC) stationary phase
  - stream of unreactive carrier gas (N_2, He) as mobile phase
  - temperature is kept constant
- **Detector**

Chromatogram
- Absorption versus time
- Area under peak gives percentage of individual component in the mixture:

$$\text{Percentage in mixture} = \frac{\text{area of peak}}{\text{total area of all peaks}}$$

Retention time
Definition: The time from injection of the sample to when the component leaves the column
-> Identify the component by comparing retention time with that of the pure substance (reference) => if identical then it is confirmed

Limitations
- Unknown compounds might not have reference retention times
- Different components might have the same retention times
- Substances with high boiling points cannot be separated

Applications
- Alcohol level in blood or urine -> evidence in court
- Composition of paints for picture restoration

Column Chromatography (CC)

- For purifying an organic product or identifying components of a mixture
- Stationary phase *(solid matrix)*: silica (SiO_2) or alumina (Al_2O_3) powder
- Mobile phase: liquid solvent (alcohol, ester)
- The sample mixtures is dissolved in a minimum of the solvent
- The mixture is run through the column and the time for each component to leave the column (retention time) is recorded
- Components separate out according to solubility and adsorption and are collected
- The Stationary phase is contained in a glass tube (simple CC*) or a steel tube (HPLC)*

Tips for Organic Synthesis and Combined Techniques Questions

What to do with the structural formula
If the product is given...
If the reactant is given...

Four tips for combined technique questions

Tips for Organic Synthesis Questions

- Circle and label the functional groups in the structural formula
- To name the compound, identify the main functional group and use this for the name stem
- The main functional group is most likely involved in the synthesis
- Recall the revision cards for each functional group remembering their characteristics, favourite reaction types, reactants, products and conditions
- Deduce from the information given (reactants, products, conditions) what is the most likely reaction to happen. *(If the carbon chain is extended during synthesis CN⁻ is likely to be a reactant)*
- If the product is given, draw lines through the molecule, especially next to side chains or functional groups, to identify fragments which could give clues to the reactants *(synthons for retrosynthesis)*
- If the reactant is given, go through all possible reactions of the different functional groups from the revision card, and choose the most suitable one according to the product or conditions given.
  Example: 4-aminophenol is the reactant
    - The amino group could react as a base (neutralization) or a nucleophile (nucleophilic substitution, condensation polymerisation)
    - The phenol group could react as an acid (neutralization) or an alcohol (esterification)
    - The phenol ring could act as an arene (electrophilic substitution, *hydrogenation)*
- Memorise diagrams of organic synthetic routes (aliphatic, aromatic, alcohols etc.) from revision guides, to familiarise yourself with the different reaction routes and conditions

Tips for Combined Techniques Questions

- First try to get the molecular formula from the elemental analysis data (-> empirical formula) and the molecular ion peak of the mass spectrum (see Year 1 revision cards)

- Identify functional groups through the information given (test tube reactions mentioned) and IR spectrum (or chemical shifts of H- and C-13 NMR).

- Draw all possible isomers according to the molecular formula and check which structure fits the NMR spectra

- Even if you do not find a structure, describe and characterise all peaks of the spectra according to the data table. This ensures you will still get marks.

The Periodic Table of Elements

(1)	(2)		(3)	(4)	(5)	(6)	(7)	(8)	(9)	(10)	(11)	(12)	(13)	(14)	(15)	(16)	(17)	0 (8) (18)
																		4.0 **He** helium 2
6.9 **Li** lithium 3	9.0 **Be** beryllium 4					1.0 **H** hydrogen 1							10.8 **B** boron 5	12.0 **C** carbon 6	14.0 **N** nitrogen 7	16.0 **O** oxygen 8	19.0 **F** fluorine 9	20.2 **Ne** neon 10
23.0 **Na** sodium 11	24.3 **Mg** magnesium 12												27.0 **Al** aluminium 13	28.1 **Si** silicon 14	31.0 **P** phosphorus 15	32.1 **S** sulfur 16	35.5 **Cl** chlorine 17	39.9 **Ar** argon 18
39.1 **K** potassium 19	40.1 **Ca** calcium 20		45.0 **Sc** scandium 21	47.9 **Ti** titanium 22	50.9 **V** vanadium 23	52.0 **Cr** chromium 24	54.9 **Mn** manganese 25	55.8 **Fe** iron 26	58.9 **Co** cobalt 27	58.7 **Ni** nickel 28	63.5 **Cu** copper 29	65.4 **Zn** zinc 30	69.7 **Ga** gallium 31	72.6 **Ge** germanium 32	74.9 **As** arsenic 33	79.0 **Se** selenium 34	79.9 **Br** bromine 35	83.8 **Kr** krypton 36
85.5 **Rb** rubidium 37	87.6 **Sr** strontium 38		88.9 **Y** yttrium 39	91.2 **Zr** zirconium 40	92.9 **Nb** niobium 41	95.9 **Mo** molybdenum 42	[98] **Tc** technetium 43	101.1 **Ru** ruthenium 44	102.9 **Rh** rhodium 45	106.4 **Pd** palladium 46	107.9 **Ag** silver 47	112.4 **Cd** cadmium 48	114.8 **In** indium 49	118.7 **Sn** tin 50	121.8 **Sb** antimony 51	127.6 **Te** tellurium 52	126.9 **I** iodine 53	131.3 **Xe** xenon 54
132.9 **Cs** caesium 55	137.3 **Ba** barium 56		138.9 **La*** lanthanum 57	178.5 **Hf** hafnium 72	180.9 **Ta** tantalum 73	183.8 **W** tungsten 74	186.2 **Re** rhenium 75	190.2 **Os** osmium 76	192.2 **Ir** iridium 77	195.1 **Pt** platinum 78	197.0 **Au** gold 79	200.6 **Hg** mercury 80	204.4 **Tl** thallium 81	207.2 **Pb** lead 82	209.0 **Bi** bismuth 83	[209] **Po** polonium 84	[210] **At** astatine 85	[222] **Rn** radon 86
[223] **Fr** francium 87	[226] **Ra** radium 88		[227] **Ac*** actinium 89	[261] **Rf** rutherfordium 104	[262] **Db** dubnium 105	[266] **Sg** seaborgium 106	[264] **Bh** bohrium 107	[277] **Hs** hassium 108	[268] **Mt** meitnerium 109	[271] **Ds** darmstadtium 110	[272] **Rg** roentgenium 111							

*Lanthanide series

140 **Ce** cerium 58	141 **Pr** praseodymium 59	144 **Nd** neodymium 60	[147] **Pm** promethium 61	150 **Sm** samarium 62	152 **Eu** europium 63	157 **Gd** gadolinium 64	159 **Tb** terbium 65	163 **Dy** dysprosium 66	165 **Ho** holmium 67	167 **Er** erbium 68	169 **Tm** thulium 69	173 **Yb** ytterbium 70	175 **Lu** lutetium 71

*Actinide series

232 **Th** thorium 90	[231] **Pa** protactinium 91	238 **U** uranium 92	[237] **Np** neptunium 93	[242] **Pu** plutonium 94	[243] **Am** americium 95	[247] **Cm** curium 96	[245] **Bk** berkelium 97	[251] **Cf** californium 98	[254] **Es** einsteinium 99	[253] **Fm** fermium 100	[256] **Md** mendelevium 101	[254] **No** nobelium 102	[257] **Lr** lawrencium 103